AN ANCHOR FOR THE SOUL

Staying Stable in Unstable Times

---

by

TIMOTHY CROSS

BA, BD, PGCE, ThD.

BELFAST, NORTHERN IRELAND
GREENVILLE, SOUTH CAROLINA

An Anchor for the Soul
© Copyright 2004 Timothy Cross

ISBN 1 84030 152 X

Ambassador Publications
a division of
Ambassador Productions Ltd.
Providence House
Ardenlee Street,
Belfast,
BT6 8QJ
Northern Ireland
www.ambassador-productions.com

Emerald House
427 Wade Hampton Blvd.
Greenville
SC 29609, USA
www.emeraldhouse.com

CONTENTS

FOREWORD

Welcome to an uplifting read! I work as a Railway Mission chaplain, which means that I travel on trains frequently. Travelling by train gives me time for preparation and study for whatever awaits me. I was given this book by the author, a good friend, who asked me whether I would be willing to write a brief 'Foreword' to it. Having read some of his previous books, I gladly agreed.

Working in the rail industry sees me wearing an identification badge similar to that worn by staff of the major railway company in my area. On seeing my 'official' badge, passengers often approach me to help them. Their questions include: 'What time is my train coming?' and 'What platform will it be on?' Whilst these were not the type of enquiries I expected to receive when I took up my role of Railway Chaplain, I can just about handle them! I know that the 'Customer Information Screens' will normally give them all the information they need, and if not, I can direct them to the 'Enquiry Desk.'

I see this book doing a similar sort of work, except giving you the necessary spiritual information for your life, as you read it chapter by chapter. The guidance offered will help you in every day situations. Like the information screens on the station concourse, here you will find information to help you - but here with spiritual application, to build you up in your faith, and enable you to face the time when maybe you find yourself 'running late' spiritually, or, worse still, bordering on a total 'faith derailment.'

This book, as the title suggests, directs the reader to the Lord Jesus Christ, Who alone is the Anchor for every soul that believes in Him. Full of Christ as it is, in reading it, you will be blessed and encouraged by its contents, built up in your faith and better equipped to travel on your life-journey ahead. Read on!

Rev Ron Keen
Railway Mission Chaplain in Wales
Barry Town Station
Broad Street
BARRY

PREFACE

In times like these, you need the Bible
In times like these, O be not idle
Be very sure, be very sure
Your anchor holds and grips the solid Rock
This Rock is Jesus, yes, He's the One
This Rock is Jesus, the only One
Be very sure, be very sure
Your anchor holds and grips the solid Rock.

Few would deny that we are living in very unstable times. The chapters which follow were actually compiled before, during and after the war in Iraq with Saddam Hussein. Here in the UK, it was felt that we faced the greatest threat to our national security and well being since the second world war.

Even in so called 'peace time' though, personal stability can be something of a rare luxury. We all face many threats to our inner peace and equilibrium. The storms of life - illness, disappointment, tragedy, redundancy etc can strike us so suddenly. Life in this world is no smooth passage and plain sailing. In the midst of our personal storms we may unconsciously sigh: 'If only we had an anchor for our souls - an anchor which keeps us from 'going under' in stormy times …'

The good news is that in the Christ of the Bible we may find the earthly and eternal security, stability and safety we crave. Christian hope in Christ is an *anchor of the soul* (Hebrews 6:19). Just as an anchor provides stability amidst the storm because it is fixed on a solid object, so the promises of God in Christ are *sure and steadfast* (Hebrews 6:19), for *Jesus Christ is the same yesterday and today and for ever* (Hebrews 13:8).

The following pages direct the reader to the sure and certain promises of God and to the ever blessed Lord Jesus Christ Himself, the Rock of Ages. Yes, life can resemble a merciless, stormy sea. Yes, our souls can feel like a fragile, vulnerable ship. But, praise God, Christian hope is an anchor - anchored firmly to Christ the solid Rock and 'hidden source of calm repose.' If you belong to Jesus *I know it is well with your soul* (3 John 2).

My prayer is that in reading the chapters which follow, you will draw near to Christ and that Christ, in His mercy, will draw near to you. I cannot promise you a trauma free life, but, directing you to the God of the Bible, I can guarantee that *He will be the stability of your times* (Isaiah 33:6). My hope is that, on completing the thirty chapters which follow, you will have been strengthened by God's grace, and so be able to sing with sincerity and joy:-

In times like these, I have a Saviour
In times like these, I have an anchor
I'm very sure, I'm very sure
My anchor holds and grips the solid Rock
This rock is Jesus, yes He's the One
This Rock is Jesus, the only One
I'm very sure, I'm very sure
My anchor holds and grips the solid Rock.

Timothy Cross
Barry, South Wales

1

AN ANCHOR FOR THE SOUL

The Anchor

Did you know that in the first century - when the Christian Faith was somewhat illicit - the anchor was a popular symbol in the Christian church? The dictionary defines an anchor as 'a heavy iron appliance with barbed arms for mooring a ship.' Pictures of anchors have been found carved in early Christian graves, places known as 'catacombs.' The anchor symbol speaks of safety and stability. Sailing on the sea has its dangers. This was especially so in the ancient world. When a storm started up and began to rage and howl, even experienced sailors would feel pangs of fear. In such a storm, a vessel would have been in great and grave danger of being shipwrecked, had they not been able to throw out an anchor. The anchor, when lowered, would grip the solid, unseen sea-bed below the surface, and then the ship would be kept safely and stably during the storm, until the danger subsided. Without an anchor, a ship would have been at the total mercy of the elements, and in dire danger of drifting to destruction.

The Anchor for the Soul

In the latter part of Hebrews chapter six in the New Testament, the writer is explaining the Christian hope, that is, the sure promises of God in Jesus Christ. Writing to Christians who lived in unstable times, he says of this hope: *We have this as a sure and steadfast anchor of the soul . . .* (Hebrews 6:19). Whilst a ship's anchor is anchored downward however, the Christian's anchor is actually anchored upward, for the same verse in full states: *We have this (hope) as a sure and steadfast anchor of the soul, a hope that enters into the inner shrine behind the curtain, where Jesus has gone as a forerunner on our behalf . . .* (Hebrews 6:19,20).

The Storms of Life and the Christian Answer

Which one of us does not sometimes feel tossed about on the stormy sea of life? Which one of us has not been made to feel our frailty and vulnerability? Our health, finances, circumstances and even our friends can seem so uncertain. No one appreciates those sudden, unexpected changes of circumstances which bring worry and apprehension. All this being so, how good it is to know Jesus as our *sure and steadfast anchor of the soul.* No earthly anchor is able or capable of giving us the earthly and eternal security which God in Christ alone can give. Notice that the Christian anchor is described as both *sure* and *steadfast.* As a sure anchor it cannot break or be disturbed or ruffled by outward circumstances. As a steadfast anchor it is reliable, trustworthy and wholly dependable. Jesus will hold us fast, and Jesus will never fail us.

Christ, the Solid Rock

If our stormy lives are the sea, and if our feeble souls are storm tossed boats upon the sea, then Hope is the anchor of the soul when it grips the solid rock of Christ Jesus. He is the hidden rock 'within the veil'. He is the One Who died for our sins to procure our eternal salvation. He is the One Who rose from the grave and ascended into heaven and now continually intercedes for His Own at the right hand of God. Read and heed the following, written by a famous Bible commentator:-

> Gospel hope is our anchor . . . In our stormy passage through this world . . . It is sure and steadfast, or else it could not keep us so. It is sure in its own nature for it is the special work of God in the soul . . . It is steadfast as it is an anchor that is cast upon the rock, the Rock of Ages. It does not seek to fasten upon the sands, but enters within the veil and fixes there upon Christ; He is the object, He is the anchor hold of the believer's hope . . .

So the big question is, at the very outset: Are you anchored to the Lord Jesus Christ? Are you trusting in the free grace of God in Christ to save your soul? Are you anchored to the finished Work of Christ on Calvary's cross for your eternal salvation? Have you come to an end of yourself and have you cast yourself wholly upon Christ - His merits and mediation - to bring you safely and surely to the safe haven of heaven itself, where the storms of this life will be gone for evermore? Christ is the Christian's anchor. What is yours?:-

> Will your anchor hold in the storms of life
> When the clouds unfold their wings of strife?
> When the strong tides lift and the cables strain
> Will your anchor drift or firm remain?
>
> Will your anchor hold in the straits of fear
> When the breakers roar and the reef is near?
> While the surgers rave and the wild winds blow
> Shall the angry waves then your bark o'er flow?
>
> Will your anchor hold in the floods of death
> When the waters cold chill your latest breath?
> On the rising tide you can never fail
> While your anchor holds within the veil

We have an anchor that keeps the soul
Steadfast and sure while the billows roll
Fastened to the rock which cannot move
Grounded firm and deep in the Saviour's love!

2

COPING WITH TRAGEDY - THE BIBLE WAY

At some point in our life, sooner or later, we will have to deal with a personal tragedy - if we have not experienced such already. The sudden loss of, for example, our health, our job or our dearest relative or friend may strike any one of us very suddenly, and seemingly without mercy. We can be sailing on the sea of life so smoothly one day, and then BANG! Tragedy strikes, leaving us absolutely paralysed, pulverised and more than a little perplexed. Christians are not immune from experiencing tragedy. We do not live in a germ-free bubble, removed from the harsh realities of life. We feel pain and hurt just the same - even though the resources of God are open for us to exploit.

The big question is then: How do we cope when life takes a different turn and appears to go desperately and hopelessly wrong? I offer the following thoughts from the Bible:-

1. God's Sovereignty

The first thing to realise is that, no matter how dire our circumstances may seem, and no matter how down our feelings get, God is still on the throne. We experience apparent 'accidents', but there are no accidents from God's perspective. He has, the Bible tells us, foreordained absolutely everything which comes to pass, with no exceptions. And His character is such, that in the life of His children at least, He is too wise to make mistakes and too loving to be unkind. The Bible says that *from Him and through Him and to Him are all things* (Romans 11:36) and He is the One Who *accomplishes all things according to the counsel of His will* (Ephesians 1:11). The Bible assures us that God is in control of absolutely every major and minor event of our lives. After all, He is God! *The LORD has established His throne in the heavens, and His kingdom rules over all* (Psalm 103:19). That this is so is confirmed by the words of the Lord Jesus when He explained: *Are not two sparrows sold for a penny? And not one of them will fall to the ground without YOUR FATHER'S WILL* (Matthew 10:29). All this is most re-assuring. God knows all about our disasters and devastations. They do not take Him by surprise or 'off guard'. Actually, looking behind all secondary causes, He is the One Who sends the harsher providences our way. Oh then to be able to take the harsher providences in the same manner as the kinder ones - and even to kiss the hand that chastises us.

2. God's Sufficiency

In Psalm 46:1 we read: *God is our refuge and strength, a very present help in trouble.* And verse 7 of the same Psalm states: *The LORD of hosts is with us, the God of Jacob is our refuge.* Think of that title *the God of Jacob.* If you know Jacob's biography, you will know that he was something of a devious trickster and 'wheeler-dealer'. The title *the God of Jacob* therefore speaks volumes about God's grace - that is, His love and favour to the undeserving and ill-deserving.

The Bible, then, assures us of God's help in and through our suffering when we reach out to Him in our need. Maybe, in His wisdom, this is why God sends us trouble and sorrow. Would we seek Him so earnestly otherwise? *Seek the LORD and His strength, seek His presence continually* (Psalm 105:4).

The Apostle Paul reported to the church at Corinth that at one time, he was in such pain through a mysterious *thorn in the flesh,* that, all he could do was to beg the Lord for its removal. *Three times I besought the Lord . . . That it should leave me* (2 Corinthians 12:8). If anyone was a devoted man of God it was Paul - yet God did not answer his prayers for deliverance. Instead, God gave him grace to cope. God promised Paul *My grace is sufficient for you, for my power is made perfect in weakness* (2 Corinthians 12:9). What a promise this is here for us to claim too. God says to us *MY GRACE IS SUFFICIENT FOR YOU.*

Of course, murmuring and complaining against our trials and tribulations is both easy and natural - yet Christians are to live on the level of the supernatural. Perish the thought that we should ever rail against God instead of seeking help from God. To whom else can we go? Where else can we even fall? The Bible says to all God's people that *The eternal God is your dwelling place, and underneath are the everlasting arms* (Deuteronomy 33:27).

3. God's Solace

Troubles, trials, tragedies et cetera . . . They make us realise just how weak we are, and just how fragile is the world in which we live. In the 'School of Adversity' we are taught that our relationship with God is our only certainly in life and death. Health fails, for our bodies break down. Friends may fail - they are only human, and fallen humans like us all. Loved ones may die - no one is immortal. Poverty may hit us, redundancy may strike with no mercy . . . But the Bible assures us *I the LORD do not change* (Malachi 3:6).

In Psalm 73, the Psalmist, at first, did what many of us are very good at. He murmured about the perceived injustices of this life, where the ungodly appear to do well, whilst God's people are made to suffer. But then he came to his right mind. Coming to his senses he thought 'theo-logically' rather than logically. He confessed to God: *Whom have I in heaven but Thee? And there is nothing upon earth that I desire besides Thee. My flesh and my heart may fail, but GOD is the strength of my heart and my portion for ever* (Psalm 73:25,26). The Psalmist knew God as his 'portion' - and, if we belong to Jesus, we may know this too. It makes all the difference in the world.

Rest in the Lord, O weary, heavy-laden
Look unto Him, your ever-present Guide
Rest in the Lord, whose Word is truth eternal
Leave all to Him, whatever may betide

Rest in the Lord, and tell Him all your sorrow
Trust in His love, so boundless, full and free
He will not leave, nor will He e'er forsake you
Rest in the Lord, and sweet your rest shall be.

3

TELL JESUS

Matthew 14:12 is a lovely little verse. The verse informs us that after John the Baptist had been cruelly and unjustly beheaded by King Herod, his grief stricken disciples *came and took the body and buried it; and they went and told Jesus.* Let us major for the next moments on those last five words: *they went and told Jesus.* 'Telling Jesus' is the essence of true prayer. We can make prayer unduly complicated. Great people are usually very inaccessible to us, yet the Christian has access to the Lord Jesus - the greatest Person ever - at any time. We can talk to Jesus. His ear is open to all our sorrows, difficulties, perplexities and problems. Just as John's bereaved disciples *went and told Jesus,* so every Christian today is privileged to be able to do the same. The verse gives us an example to emulate.

Jesus and our sorrows

It is good to be able to tell Jesus our sorrows. He is the most sympathetic Saviour. He has walked the paths we have walked, sin apart. Isaiah 53:3 describes Him as *a man of sorrows and acquainted with grief.* Those feeling 'knocked about' by this world need to be handled sensitively and with great care. Jesus is infinite in sensitivity and care. Matthew 12:20 says of Him *He will not break a bruised reed or quench a smouldering wick.* In Matthew 11:29 Jesus tells us that He is *gentle and lowly in heart.* Truly, in our sorrow, it is good to 'tell Jesus'.

Prayer changes us

Telling Jesus changes us. Burdens can feel so heavy, and little 'niggles' can be so annoying and irksome. Praying to Jesus changes us. We may unburden our burdens on Him, the great Burden Bearer. *Cast all your anxieties on Him, for He cares about you* (1 Peter 5:7). Certain subjects of conversation are 'no go areas' with us, even with our close family and friends. Thankfully, there are no 'no go areas' when it comes to prayer. Hence Paul could exhort in Philippians 4:6: *Have no anxiety about anything, but in everything by prayer and supplication with thanksgiving, let your requests be made known to God.* No problem is too great for omnipotence. None of our burdens will over-burden the Lord Jesus. And nothing that bothers us is too small or trivial for Him either. John's disciples *went and told Jesus.* They were grief stricken, but in telling Jesus we can be sure that their sorrows were soothed, their turmoil was calmed and their souls restored.

To Whom are we talking?

Telling Jesus is taking matters right 'to the top.' Jesus is almighty to change things, and Jesus can minister His all-sufficient grace. When you talk to Jesus, remember just Who He is. He is the Son of God and God the Son. Remember that He actually created this vast universe, for *all things were made through Him, and without Him was not anything made that was made* (John 1:3). There is no higher authority to which you can take your humble requests than Jesus. He *is the head of all rule and authority* (Colossians 2:10). True prayer therefore is the most practical step we can take.

Jesus is a faithful Friend

Telling Jesus is telling things to a faithful Friend. The Bible says *A friend loves at all times, and a brother is born for adversity* (Proverbs 17:17). Similarly, *There are friends who pretend to be friends, but there is a friend who sticks closer than a brother* (Proverbs 18:24). Jesus is such a Friend. He never turns any one away. He stated *He who comes to Me I will not cast out* (John 6:37). He has never and will never fail or forsake anyone. His unbreakable promise is *I will never fail you nor forsake you* (Hebrews 13:5).

Jesus' Calvary love

Lastly, remember that telling Jesus is telling One Who loves us with a love stronger than death and hell. Telling Jesus is telling the One Who has procured our eternal salvation. He *gave Himself for our sins* (Galatians 1:4). *Christ loved us and gave Himself up for us* (Ephesians 5:2). He *loved me and gave Himself for me* (Galatians 2:20). The love of Jesus was demonstrated supremely when He died in our place to save us from eternal condemnation and procure for us an eternal home in heaven, for ever saved and for ever safe from all that ails us and brings us down.

Tell Jesus

They went and told Jesus (Matthew 14:12). It is prayer at its most basic, and surely the best and wisest action that any one of us can ever take.

> What a Friend we have in Jesus
> All our sins and griefs to bear
> What a privilege to carry
> Everything to God in prayer
> O what peace we often forfeit
> O what needless pain we bear
> All because we do not carry
> Everything to God in prayer

Have we trials and temptations?
Is there trouble anywhere?
We should never be discouraged
Take it to the Lord in prayer
Can we find a Friend so faithful
Who will all our sorrows share?
Jesus knows our every weakness
Take it to the Lord in prayer

Blessed Jesus, Thou hast promised
Thou wilt all our burdens bear
May we ever Lord be bringing
All to Thee in earnest prayer
Soon in glory, bright, unclouded
There will be no need for prayer
Rapture, praise and endless worship
Shall be our sweet portion there.

4

STEALING : WHAT CANNOT BE STOLEN

Two of my friends have recently had the ghastly experience of having their homes burgled. Such an occurrence comes as a dreadful shock. It is not so much the inconvenience of having household articles stolen, they have said, but rather the thought that a totally unknown stranger has invaded and looked around uninvited.

Recovering from having both our privacy and security totally violated can take a long time. Sometimes people never get over it, and are so unsettled that, sadly, they have to move home.

God's Law

Crimes such as burglary are one symptom of the ungodly days in which we live. I was astonished once when I heard that an ordained 'Christian' minister was reported on the radio as saying that stealing, under some circumstances, is justified. I just hope that the Reverend gentleman never has his house burgled and ends up eating his words.

The eighth commandment, given by God to Moses on Mount Sinai - a commandment which is valid for all time - is crystal clear:

You shall not steal (Exodus 20:15). The commandment teaches a basic respect for other people and their property, and 'the lawful procuring and furthering the wealth and outward estate of ourselves and others' (*Shorter Catechism*). It just goes to show what happens when society and the individuals comprising it turn away from God. Turning away from God means turning away from the law of God - and turning away from the law of God means exchanging the law of heaven for the lawlessness of hell. The only alternative to God's law is anarchy. It matters intensely then what we believe - the liberal, laissez faire outlook of some ministers and teachers today notwithstanding. What we believe affects how we behave. When churches, communities and individuals lose the fear of God, all hell literally breaks loose. We have, to use the words of Hosea 8:7, *sown the wind and reaped the whirlwind.*

The Christian's Secure Possessions

Whilst thinking about my friends' harsh providences, Hebrews 10:34 came into my mind. It is a verse which causes us much heart searching - wondering how we would act and react in similar circumstances. In Hebrews 10:34, the writer wrote to his Jewish Christian friends, reporting how *you joyfully accepted the plundering of your property, since you knew that you yourselves had a better posses-sion and an abiding one.* Did you catch that? *you joyfully accepted the plundering of your property, since you knew that you yourselves had a better possession and an abiding one.* The verse suggests that those early believers were so taken up with and infatuated by the eternal riches they had in Christ, that the loss of their earthly wealth and possessions was of no consequence to them, and hardly affected them at all. Oh to be like that! To quote the chorus:-

Turn your eyes upon Jesus
Look full in His wonderful face
And the things of earth will go strangely dim
In the light of His glory and grace.

Truth be told, even the richest man in the world does not actually own anything. None of us do. One day we will have to leave everything we have behind us and never be able to reclaim it. Shrouds have no pockets! It is only at that time that we will know how truly rich we are, and what is of eternal value.

Treasures in Heaven

Our possessions in this world are more fragile than we think. The shock of a burglary wakes us up to this. If we know our Bibles though, we can state that nothing of value can ever be stolen from us. (This is not to say that criminals will escape God's punishment, or that they should not be caught and punished.)

The Lord Jesus gives us the following exhortation: *Do not lay up for yourselves treasures on earth, where moth and rust consume and where thieves break in and steal, but lay up for yourselves treasures in heaven, where neither moth nor rust consumes and where thieves do not break in and steal. For where your treasure is, there will your heart be also* (Matthew 6:19-21).

One who lived this out in practice was the apostle Paul. He could put his hand on his heart and testify *I count everything as loss because of the surpassing worth of knowing Christ Jesus my Lord. For His sake I have suffered the loss of all things and count them as refuse, in order that I may gain Christ . . .* (Philippians 3:8). Paul was concerned only with *the unreachable riches of Christ* (Ephesians 3:8). Possessing these Riches puts earthly riches - or the lack or loss of them - into their true perspective.

Burglary - just like illness and the loss of a job - comes as a rude awakening. Yet such unwelcome providences test us and reveal our true values - where our hearts really are. Do we live so exclusively for the things of time that the things of eternity are put on the back burner? Are we so taken up with the things of the world - legitimate and illegitimate - that we have become oblivious to the things of lasting, eternal worth?

Only those who know Jesus, and rejoice in the eternal salvation which He has procured by His death and resurrection can claim to really own anything. Nothing else lasts. As the hymn goes:-

> Fading is the worldling's pleasure
> All his boasted pomp and show
> Solid joys and lasting treasure
> None but Zion's children know.

Or as Peter put it:- *Blessed be the God and Father of our Lord Jesus Christ! By His great mercy we have been born anew to a living hope through the resurrection of Jesus Christ from the dead, and to an inheritance which is imperishable, undefiled and unfading, kept in heaven for you . . .* (1 Peter 1:3,4).

> We sing the praise of Him Who died
> Of Him Who died upon the cross
> The sinner's hope, let men deride
> For this we count the world but loss.

5

THE DIVINE REFINER

One of the more unusual pictures which the Bible uses to describe Almighty God is that of a silver refiner. Proverbs 17:3 states *The crucible is for silver, and the furnace is for gold, and the LORD tries hearts.* Similarly, in Malachi 3:3 we read that God will *sit as a refiner and purifier of silver.*

Refining Silver

The silver refining occupation was well known in Bible times. Sitting at his work, the silver refiner would fan his charcoal fire, looking intently into the crucible, waiting to see a clear reflection of his face in the molten metal below him. When his face appeared clearly, he would be satisfied. The heat had done its job. The dross and impurities had been burned away, and the metal was now useable and useful. It could be used to make something special:- *Take away the dross from the silver and the smith has material for a vessel* (Proverbs 25:4).

Refining People

Refining silver is one thing, but the Bible, in our opening verse, suggests that God refines His people. In His peculiar love, He turns up the heat on them. This is one of the ways in which we may view the various trials that providence sends into our lives. The trials are part of the process of sanctification, and will not be complete until a clear reflection of the face of Christ is seen in us. God refines His people. He does so, not to save them, for God's people are already saved - saved by the Christ Who went through the incomparable sufferings of Calvary on their behalf. No. God refines His people to sanctify them - to get rid of the dross that hinders our usefulness; to get rid of those blemishes that mar our Christ likeness. The process is a long, slow and painful one for sure - and it will never be completed in this life. Yet it is reassuring to know that our God of infinite love, wisdom and righteousness is the One controlling the temperature of our trials. He knows just what we need. It is wise then to submit to God's refining and co-operate with Him as best we can.

An ageing Paul wrote the following to young Timothy in 2 Timothy 2:21 ff. *If any one purifies himself from what is ignoble, then he will be a vessel for noble use, consecrated and useful to the master of the house, ready for any good work. So shun youthful passions and aim at righteousness, faith, love and peace, along with those who call upon the Lord from a pure heart.* Oh to be such a vessel: a vessel fit for the Master's use - useable, useful, and used; glorifying to God and a channel of His blessing to others.

No pain, no gain

The crucible is for silver, and the furnace is for gold, and the LORD tries hearts (Proverbs 17:3). No one would ever suggest that being in God's crucible is pleasant. It may be necessary, for sure, as sin is so deeply ingrained in us. It may also have such a wonderful end result and be so worthwhile overall. Yet when the heat is really turned up on us, our Christian maturity or otherwise is really revealed.

Often, it is not so much how we act, but how we re-act, that reveals our true characters.

The painful nature of being in God's crucible, along with its beneficial end result, was known well by the writer to the epistle to the Hebrews. Changing the metaphor to that of a loving father being 'cruel to be kind', and disciplining his son, he wrote the following - words which are the definitive statement concerning divine chastisement:-

My son, do not regard lightly the discipline of the Lord, nor lose courage when you are punished by Him. For the Lord disciplines him whom He loves, and chastises every son whom He receives . . . God is treating you as sons; for what son is there whom his father does not discipline? . . . He disciplines us for our good, that we may share His holiness. For the moment all discipline seems painful rather than pleasant; later it yields the peaceful fruit of righteousness to those who have been trained by it (Hebrews 11:5 ff.).

God moves in a mysterious way

Who then would have thought that trials and difficulties are an evidence of God's love? God is refining His silver. He will have His way. He has not finished with us yet. *The LORD will fulfil His purpose for me; Thy steadfast love, O LORD endures for ever. Do not forsake the work of Thy hands* (Psalm 138:8). *He Who began a good work in you will bring it to completion at the day of Jesus Christ* (Philippians 1:6).

When 'sore troubles' come your way then, seek the Lord and His grace. And remember that our Father in heaven is a silver refiner par excellence!

> When through fiery trials thy pathway shall lie
> My grace all-sufficient shall be thy supply
> The flame shall not hurt thee, I only design
> Thy dross to consume, and thy gold to refine.

6

THE SEAL OF THE HOLY SPIRIT

The Holy Trinity

The full-orbed Christian doctrine of God takes us to the doctrine of
the Trinity. This states that the One true God has existed eternally in
the three Persons of God the Father, Son and Holy Spirit. The *Shorter
Catechism* puts it this way:-

> There are three Persons in the God-head; the Father,
> the Son and the Holy Ghost, and these three are one
> God, the same in substance, equal in power and glory.

The Holy Spirit

Of these three Divine Persons, the Holy Spirit has been,
historically, the somewhat lower in profile member of the Trinity in
Christian public teaching. Apart from the Holy Spirit's ministry
though, we could never be saved at all. It is the Holy Spirit of God
Who brings all the blessings of God to the human soul. Chief among

His work is the effectual application of the work of Christ on the Cross to our souls. This work, carried out in our innermost hearts, convicts us of our sin and need and enables us to believe in Jesus. In believing in Jesus we receive the salvation He has procured, and as a result are filled with that unique joy and peace in believing, which only God's people know.

The Holy Spirit's Seal

A largely neglected aspect of the Holy Spirit's blessed ministry to the Christian is that of 'sealing.' Yet this 'sealing' is most definitely taught in the Bible. It is one of the Christian's new birth rights!

Paul wrote this to the Christians at Ephesus, and by implication, to all Christians: *you . . . who have heard the Word of truth, the Gospel of your salvation, and have believed in Him, were sealed with the promised Holy Spirit* (Ephesians 1:13). This then is one of the distinguishing marks of a Christian. A Christian has been *sealed with the promised Holy Spirit.* Paul reiterates this in chapter 4 verse 30 of the same letter to the Ephesians when he exhorts: *do not grieve the Holy Spirit of God, in Whom you were sealed for the day of redemption.* What then is this invisible, yet nonetheless very real seal? A commentator on these verses clarified it this way:-

> In the ancient world visible seals were used to attest as genuine (c.f. our trademarks), to mark ownership and to keep secure.

The seal of the Holy Spirit is proof that we genuinely belong to Jesus. In Romans 8:9 Paul wrote *Any one who does not have the Spirit of Christ does not belong to Him.* The seal of the Holy Spirit is also the mark of God's ownership of us - He not only made us, but He has also purchased us, for we have been bought by the blood of His Son. The seal of the Holy Spirit is also evidence of our security. Our three enemies, namely the world, the flesh and the devil are far more powerful than we are. Yet they are no match for the Spirit of God dwelling in us. He will keep us safely, and bring us surely and securely to the Glory land, saved to sin no more. We are *sealed for the day of redemption,* and, praise God, we cannot be unsealed.

In Bible times, 'sealing' was a well known practice. Paul's original readers would have needed no explanation of what he meant. A booklet I have entitled *The Bible Comes to Life* - a work explaining the Bible in the light of its middle-eastern setting - explains how, in the first century:-

> Letters, books, documents and other possessions were sealed to indicate ownership, authority or the value of an article. Paul uses this old custom of sealing to show how the believer has been purchased and paid for by the blood of Christ.

2 Corinthians 1:22 tells us that God *has put His <u>seal</u> upon us and given us His Spirit in our hearts as a guarantee. The Bible Comes to Life* also has an interesting paragraph under the heading of a 'Corn Seal'. The corn seal, it says, was:-

> Made of wood and measures about 48x24x2 cms. On one side the monogram of the owner is deeply cut while on the other side is fixed the handle. When a man has purchased a quantity of corn it is placed in a heap which he proceeds to seal carefully by pressing his monogram upon it. This is to warn all who pass by that the corn has been purchased and paid for and is the property of the person whose seal is upon it. Later the man will send a servant with a donkey to collect or redeem it in his name.

So do you see what Paul meant when he referred to the Holy Spirit's sealing of the Christian? - *sealed for the day of redemption.* Having been purchased by the blood of Christ we belong to Him. He bought us, and currently owns us, and is soon going to come and collect us and take us to Himself. What a day that will be! Jesus said: *'I will come again and will take you to Myself, that where I am you may be also'* (John 14:3).

The Pledge of Glory

The last book of the Bible - the book of Revelation - was written amidst the most troublesome, violent and unstable days. If anyone should have believed that a Christian could not be certain of salvation, surely the author of that book, the aged John the Apostle, should have. But no! God gave John a vision. He was enabled to see life from a divine perspective. *I saw another angel . . . With the seal of the living God, and he called with a loud voice . . . 'Do not harm the earth or the sea or the trees, till we have sealed the servants of our God upon their foreheads.' And I heard the number of the sealed, a hundred and forty four thousand . . .* (Revelation 7:2 ff.). A hundred and forty four thousand? It is a symbolic number. There were twelve tribes of Israel, and there were twelve Apostles. 12x12=144. It refers to God's true Church - the large number of people from all ages who belong to Jesus. They alone have God's seal upon them, and so they are saved and safe. They are sealed with the Holy Spirit. This being so, whatever their lot in this world, they will yet be a glorified people. They are destined to enjoy the presence of God for all eternity.

So, Christian. If you have never done so before, bow your head at this very moment, and thank God for the blessed sealing of His Holy Spirit.

7

TEARS

Our subject for this chapter is not a pleasant one. It is the subject of tears. Surprisingly today, when almost anything goes and censorship has never been laxer, tears are still something of a taboo subject. We do not talk about them. Of course, we would all like to avoid them completely in practice as well as in theory, but somehow we cannot. Tears are part and parcel of being human. The Psalmist spoke for everyone when he wrote *My tears have been my food day and night* (Psalm 42:3). Tears are with us from infancy until old age. Tears respect no one, for their bitter, salty flavour will be tasted by everyone at some time, whether rich or poor, religious or irreligious, Muslim or Jew, Protestant or Catholic.

When I lived in the troubled, sectarian city of Belfast, Northern Ireland, I sometimes wondered how many gallons of tears had been shed there during the 'troubles'. Yet tears are not confined to Belfast, even if they were a little more higher in profile there. Tears show that we are more than just animals. Animals do not cry. We do, for tears are the language and the expression of the human soul. Tears come upon us for various reasons, but usually when we are right on the brink - on the edge of extremity, bordering on rock bottom, verging on despair with no human way out.

The Sympathetic Saviour

Did you know that the shortest verse in the Bible is John 11:35? John 11:35, in full, reads simply: *Jesus wept*. Because *Jesus wept* we can state categorically that our God, in Christ, knows what it is like to be human. The Christian God is no mere remote deity. Jesus knew and felt the inner anguish which we sometimes experience. He also cried. It is comforting to know. Our God is a God of infinite compassion. Hence His words to a distressed King Hezekiah, thousands of years ago: *'I have heard your prayer, I have seen your tears'* (Isaiah 35:5).

The University of Sorrow

No one relishes tears. Yet they do teach us to seek God. They do force us out of any cosy, comfortable complacency, and make us look up, above and beyond this unreliable world. Our extremity is God's opportunity - our insufficiency will prove His all-sufficiency.

Tears also teach us the needed grace of human sympathy. *Rejoice with those who rejoice, weep with those who weep* (Romans 12:15) exhorts Paul. It is so easy to accidentally hurt others by our thoughtlessness. It is so easy to be blasé, and behave like the proverbial 'bull in a china shop.' But how much do tears tenderise us. Tears make us more careful and prayerful people - more in fact like the Lord Jesus Christ Whom we follow. Jesus is described as *a man of sorrows and acquainted with grief* (Isaiah 53:3). How different the world would be if every Christian exhibited Christ-like tenderness. It was written of Him *a bruised reed He will not break, and a dimly burning wick He will not quench* (Isaiah 42:2).

When tears will be no more

The good news is however, that the God of the Bible is the great tear-dryer. *The LORD God will wipe away tears from all faces* (Isaiah

25:8). The last book of the Bible, with its enthralling glimpses and descriptions of the glory to be, includes the significant detail that *God will wipe away every tear from their eyes* (Revelation 7:17). Is that not music to your ears? It certainly is to mine!

The Ultimate Cause of and Remedy for Tears

Is there anything worse than tears? The Bible would say that there is. Biblically, sin is worse than tears, as sin is the ultimate cause of all tears, sorrow and pain. Before sin entered the scene way back in Eden's Garden, not one tear of distress or sorrow had ever fallen to the ground - but how all that changed with the entrance of sin into the world. Sin therefore is even worse than tears.

The Christian Gospel joyfully proclaims a remedy for sin and its consequent tears. On the cross, we read of Jesus, that *He Himself bore our sins in His body on the tree* (1 Peter 2:24). Yes, Jesus, the sinless One, bore our sins, and God's righteous punishment upon them, so that whoever believes in Him may one day bask in God's presence for evermore, and never cry again.

What a contrast there is between heaven and hell. In heaven, as we have seen, *God will wipe away every tear from their eyes.* In hell, we read, *men will weep and gnash their teeth* (Matthew 8:12) - and both heaven and hell are eternal. No words can describe the awfulness of hell's weeping and remorse - no matter how tearless one's existence may have been here on earth. Also, no words can describe the absolute delightfulness of heaven - no matter how tearful one's existence may have been here on earth. One breath of Paradise will compensate superabundantly for all the adverse winds of earth which blew our way and caused us tears. *I consider that the sufferings of this present time are not worth comparing with the glory that is to be revealed to us* (Romans 8:18).

How to be sure of heaven

The only way to heaven is through Jesus and His death on the cross. Did you know that the thought of His impending cross once moved the Lord Jesus to tears? *In the days of His flesh, Jesus offered up prayers and supplications with loud cries and tears, to Him Who was able to save Him from death* (Hebrews 5:7). His death though was not in vain. His death is our life, His shed blood brings us forgiveness, His pain brings us Paradise, His earthly tears caused the eternal triumph of all who are united to Him by saving faith.

Do you belong to Jesus? If you do, take heart. You are heading for glory. There, Almighty God, in an act of infinite compassion and sensitivity, has promised that He will wipe away every tear from your eyes - fully, finally and for ever!

Our God has fixed the happy day
When the last tear shall dim our eyes
When He will wipe all tears away
And fill our hearts with glad surprise
To hear His voice, to see His face
And know the riches of His grace.

8

'THE SHADOW OF THY WINGS'

The story is told of a farmer who lost everything he had through a devastating fire. Walking through the burnt remains of his barn that had been, he kicked a charred heap on the floor. Lo and behold, out ran twelve beautiful chicks! They had been sheltering under the wings of their mother. She had braved the fire to save them. It is true, that when any dangerous or threatening circumstances occur, a mother hen will call her chicks and stretch out her wings over them. How glad they are to run to her, and find refuge, protection and safety under her wings, until the danger has passed.

The Shadow of Thy Wings

In Psalm 36:7, the Psalmist addresses these words to God: *How precious is Thy steadfast love, O God! The children of men take refuge in the shadow of Thy wings.* For this chapter, let us consider that expression *the shadow of Thy wings.* It is an expression which tells us of the refuge available to us, not in something relatively frail and feeble, but in Almighty God Himself.

The God of the Bible, of course, has no physical wings as such. The expression is a metaphorical one, for the New Testament informs us that *God is spirit* (John 4:24). Whilst the expression is picture language though, it nevertheless describes a refuge and reality that is absolutely real. For in Almighty God, we may find both eternal and earthly refuge and repose.

The Background

In the 'holy of holies' in the ancient tabernacle, the omnipresent God presenced Himself in a very real and particular way. This being so, who would dare to enter into the holy of holies and approach this thrice holy Being? No mortal. No mortal that is, except the high priest, and he but once a year, on the Day of Atonement. Access to God then was only on the basis of animal sacrifice - blood atonement. In the holy of holies there stood the Ark of the Covenant, within which God's holy law was placed. Overshadowing the ark were two cherubim, whose wings covered and overshadowed the ark. It was upon these wings - a place known as the 'mercy seat' - that the high priest would sprinkle the blood of atoning sacrifice. The blood signified words to this effect:- 'You, O God, are holy. We, O God, are sinners in your sight, unfit for Your presence. We deserve to die for our sins, and be banished from You. But thank you Lord God for providing and accepting the death of this innocent animal in my place, so that my sins can be forgiven, I may be saved from Your righteous anger, and be enabled to come into Your presence.'

Eternal Safety

With the above in mind, think again of our verse: *The children of men take refuge in the shadow of Thy wings.* How can we ever face God, knowing that we have failed to live up to His holy demands? We have all broken His law. How can we ever face up to God's wrath on the judgement day? The answer is: Only by taking refuge in the shadow of His wings. Only by fleeing to the mercy seat He has graciously given. Only by fleeing to the Lord Jesus, Who on Calvary, offered up His sinless life and shed His precious blood as the all sufficient, eternal, atoning sacrifice for sins. As a little chick finds safety from the storm under its mother's wing, we too may find eternal safety from the storm of God's wrath in Jesus, the only Saviour of sinners. The Bible tells us that it is Jesus Who delivers us from the wrath to come. The Bible assures us that *There is therefore now no condemnation for those who are in Christ Jesus* (Romans 8:1). He is our eternal refuge - yet He is also the earthly refuge of all those who belong to Him too:-

Earthly Refuge

The children of men take refuge in the shadow of Thy wings. Where can we go when the storms of life howl at our heart's door? There is an earthly refuge - *in the shadow of Thy wings.* When our friends fail us, when our good health gives way, when some tragedy or sudden calamity assails us making it feel like our whole world has caved in . . . There is a place of earthly refuge - *in the shadow of Thy wings.*

> From every stormy wind that blows
> From every swelling tide of woes
> There is a calm, a safe retreat
> Tis found beneath the mercy seat
>
> There is a place where Jesus sheds
> The oil of gladness on our heads
> A place than all beside more sweet
> It is the blood-stained mercy seat.

The Deity of Christ

In Matthew 23:37, Jesus' heart-felt words are recorded as follows: *'O Jerusalem, Jerusalem. How often would I have gathered your children together as a hen gathers her brood under her wings . . .'* In the Old Testament, the expression 'the shadow of thy wings' was used of none other than the Lord Jehovah. Here though, Jesus applies it to Himself. So, outstandingly, we have here one of the lesser known evidences of the deity of Christ, that is, that Jesus Christ is God - co-equal with the Father and the Holy Spirit. As He is God, the safety and security which we may enjoy in Jesus just cannot be compared. In Him alone we may find the eternal safety of eternal salvation from our sins, and earthly refuge and solace in and amidst all the storms of life, confident that His grace is more than sufficient for all our needs.

The children of men take refuge in the shadow of Thy wings. Is that where you find refuge too?

> Safe in the arms of Jesus
> Safe on His gentle breast
> There by His love o'er shadowed
> Sweetly my soul shall rest
>
> Safe in the arms of Jesus
> Safe from corroding care
> Safe from the world's temptations
> Sin cannot harm me there
>
> Jesus my heart's dear refuge
> Jesus Who died for me
> Firm on the Rock of Ages
> Ever my trust shall be.

9

9/11

Who could ever forget September 11th, 2001? '9/11', as it is widely known, was the day when three thousand and forty five people suddenly lost their lives in a cruel, calculated terrorist attack in New York. The ramifications and repercussions of the day are still with us. It was a day which changed the world. The very mention of 9/11 triggers off in us our recollections of where we were and what we were doing at the time, and the mixed emotions of disbelief, numbness, sadness and outrage we then felt.

Writing as a Bible-believing Christian, and not as a politician, I ask the question: Does the Bible cast any light on that black day in the autumn of 2001? It does indeed:-

The Sovereignty of God

The Bible encourages us to see God's providence behind absolutely everything that happens, with no exceptions. Behind 'secondary causes' - even the evil intentions of wicked men - there yet lies the sovereign will of God. The *Shorter Catechism* reminds us that 'The decrees of God are His eternal purpose, according to the counsel of His will, whereby, for His Own glory, He has foreordained whatsoever comes to pass.'

We are forced to admit our limitations here. In fact, confessing our ignorance is a mark of intelligence. God's ways are sometimes beyond us. After all, He is God! We, being finite creatures cannot always comprehend the infinite God. We can say though that He knows what He is doing, and He is worthy of our trust. *My thoughts are not your thoughts, neither are your ways My ways,' says the LORD* (Isaiah 55:8). *How unsearchable are His judgements, and how inscrutable His ways* (Romans 11:33). God is infinitely different. *There is none holy like the LORD, there is none besides Thee* (1 Samuel 2:2).

The Sin of Man

The Bible diagnoses all the sorrow and disharmony of the world as being a consequence of human sin. Sin puts us out of fellowship with our Maker and each other. Sin manifests itself in myriads of painful, destructive ways. Romans 3 tells us that *all men, both Jews and Greeks, are under the power of sin* (v.9), and then - as we remember 9/11 - goes on to say that one of the consequences of sin is this: *Their feet are swift to shed blood, in their paths are ruin and misery, and the way of peace they do not know* (vv. 15,16).

As sinners, we are all in need of salvation. And it is the Christian Gospel which *is the power of God for salvation to everyone who has faith* (Romans 1:16).

The Fragility of Life

Days such as September 11th, 2001, remind us that life is brief and fragile, eternity is ever near, and this world is, at best, very uncertain. *You do not know about tomorrow. What is your life? For you are a mist that appears for a little time and then vanishes* (James 4:14). The shocks of this world can act as a wake-up call to us. We cannot assume a tomorrow or a next week. How vital it is therefore to be right with our Maker, as we could face Him at any time. The only way to be right with our Maker is to know that our sins are forgiven. The only way to be sure that our sins are forgiven is to trust in the Lord Jesus, God's Son, the Saviour of sinners. Decisions in time affect eternity. Decisions on earth affect whether we will spend eternity in heaven or in hell. Hence 2 Corinthians 6:2: *Behold, now is the acceptable time; behold, now is the day of salvation.*

In Luke 13, the Lord Jesus was asked about a certain tower which fell on eighteen people, killing them instantly. Jesus here refused to get involved in the kind of theological speculation and debate which 9/11 brought in its wake. Instead, He gave the stark warning: *'Unless you repent, you will all likewise perish'* (v.5).

The Comfort of God

Amidst the difficulties, perplexities, disappointments and even the devastations of this life, Christians have a resource of which the world knows nothing. We have a God to Whom we can turn. *The LORD is good, a stronghold in the day of trouble; He knows those who take refuge in Him* (Nahum 1:7). *God is our refuge and strength, a very present help in trouble. Therefore we will not fear though the earth should change, though the mountains shake in the heart of the sea; though the waters roar and foam, though the mountains tremble with its tumult* (Psalm 46:1-3).

The Promise of Peace to Come

Christians know - on the authority of the Bible - that this world will not remain the way it is now for ever. One day, God will right all wrongs. He will punish evil doers eternally, and bring in His Kingdom of everlasting righteousness and peace. We pray for this future blessing every time we pray *Thy Kingdom come.*

The ultimate goal of all history is the Second Coming of the Lord Jesus Christ. And when He comes again, there will be cosmic redemption. *According to His promise we wait for new heavens and a new earth in which righteousness dwells* (2 Peter 3:13). *They shall beat their swords into plough shares, and their spears into pruning hooks; nation shall not lift up sword against nation, neither shall they learn war any more* (Isaiah 2:4).

September 11th - 9/11. It is a day which will be for ever etched upon world history and in our minds and memories. Strange to report, but I have heard unbelievers audaciously railing against Almighty God for that human tragedy. How we react to devastation reveals much about the state of our souls. We either turn against God, or we seek Him more earnestly - cleaving to His promises and asking Him for help and comfort, being reassured from the Bible that He is actually working all things out for our good, and that nothing can separate us from the love of God in Christ Jesus our Lord.

As you read this though, I am aware that you may have your own version of 9/11 - a particularly sad and devastating day when your circumstances changed suddenly, and your whole world caved in. If so, may the following be balm to your troubled soul:-

O Child of God, this grief
That bows your spirit low
Is yours but half, for Christ Himself
Still shares His peoples' woe

His wisdom planned it out
Then bore it on His heart
Till gently on your untried back
Love laid the lesser part

So take it with all joy
Together bear the cross
For while you suffer, He distils
A heaven from your loss

Beneath His secret will
Subscribe with ready pen
Add to this sorrow God has sent
A resolute 'Amen'

Each day spend out in faith
Nor prove His labour vain
Cast still on Christ the pressing weight
Who only can sustain.

10

'HIS EYE IS ON THE SPARROW, AND I KNOW HE CARES ABOUT ME'

The first three verses of Psalm 84 read:- *How lovely is Thy dwelling place, O LORD of hosts! My soul longs, yea faints for the courts of the LORD; my heart and flesh sing for joy to the living God. Even the sparrow finds a home, and the swallow a nest for herself, where she may lay her young, at Thy altars, O LORD of hosts, my King and my God.*

Ornithology is not my brief. But for this chapter, I should like us to consider the little sparrow alluded to in the verses above. The Psalmist in this Psalm expresses His intense longing for God's courts. We all, at some time, get such 'longings'- longings for favourite and familiar people and places, when we are far away from them. The Welsh language, interestingly, has the untranslatable word 'hiraeth' for such a feeling. Smitten by a longing for God's house in Jerusalem though, the Psalmist recalled noticing how some cheeky little sparrow had had the audacity to make its home there - there in the holy temple of Jerusalem itself.

The Sparrow

In the Bible, the sparrow - such a relatively tiny, insignificant little bird - teaches us much about God's intimate care and concern for you and me. Jesus said: *'Are not two sparrows sold for a penny? And not one of them will fall to the ground without your Father's will. But even the hairs of your head are numbered. Fear not therefore, you are of more value than many sparrows'* (Matthew 10:28-31).

Think of a little sparrow then, and let it remind you of just how precious you are to God. How can anyone begin to put a price tag on the value of your soul? If you are a Christian, we can say that it cost the death of the Lord Jesus to redeem your soul. If the death of an insignificant sparrow though is not by chance, employ logic and 'theo-logic', and argue from the lesser to the greater. If a sparrow dies, not by chance, but because of God's ordinance, how much more can we rule out any notion of 'chance' in our lives. We are made in the image of God. We are redeemed by the blood of His Son. He loves us with an everlasting love. God's providence extends to every single area of our lives, major and minor, with no exceptions. How we need to trust Him more than we do! If His eye is on the sparrow, how much more can we trust His Fatherly kindness through all the ups and downs of life. Jesus said elsewhere: *'Look at the birds of the air: they neither reap nor gather into barns, and yet your heavenly Father feeds them. Are you not of more value than they?'* (Matthew 6:26).

The Sanctuary

Notice from our opening verses, that the sparrow had found *a home. A home.* This begs the following evangelistic question: Are you at home? By that, I do not mean physically, but spiritually. You see, apart from trusting in Jesus as our own, personal Saviour, we are all lost, and consequently unsettled and away from our true home. It is no wonder that this will make us feel ill at ease in this life and irreparably so in the next. Jesus said of Himself *'The Son of Man came to seek and to save the lost'* (Luke 19:10), and once told a parable which was to become famous as the 'Parable of the Prodigal Son.' In this parable, a rebellious son, having tasted the bitterness of the unhappiness and bitterness which resulted from straying from his father's home, finally came to his senses and returned home. There he was received with open arms and great joy. And what a picture this gives us of the Father-heart of God, and the wideness of His love as He invites straying sinners to come home, where they truly belong. In Psalm 84, the sparrow found a home in God's house. We too may have a home in God's heart, when we trust in Jesus. His death on the cross forgives all our sins and restores us to fellowship with God, both now and for ever.

The Seeker

Notice finally that our opening text says that *the sparrow finds a home*. This suggests that the sparrow's ideal and happy accommodation did not just happen, but rather came about as a result of much seeking. And did you know that this is the same as regards our relationship with God? The Bible reveals that God blesses earnest seekers. Consider, and be encouraged from what one of the ancient prophets wrote:- *Seek the LORD while He may be found, call upon Him while He is near, let the wicked forsake his way, and the unrighteous man his thoughts, let him return to the LORD, that He may have mercy on him, and to our God, for He will abundantly pardon* (Isaiah 55:6,7).

So give yourself no rest until you have found your heart's rest and true home in the Lord Jesus Christ. Then you will out-sing even the sparrow! You will then concur with the next verse of the Psalm we have considered: *Blessed are those who dwell in Thy house, ever singing Thy praise* (Psalm 84:4).

The sparrow found its home. Have you?

Come unto Me ye weary
And I will give you rest
O blessed voice of Jesus
Which comes to hearts oppressed
It tells of benediction
Of pardon, grace and peace
Of joy that has no ending
Of love which cannot cease.

11

COPING WITH ILLNESS

I am writing this chapter whilst recovering from Pleurisy. Pleurisy, the hospital consultant told me, is 'an inflammation of the membrane enclosing the lungs.' At its height, it felt like a great big concrete block had been dropped on my chest. I thought that Pleurisy was something confined to the Victorian era. I now know better!

When illness strikes

None of us relish being ill and laid aside from normal living. Being human though, it is highly likely that we have been ill, we are currently ill, or we will be ill at sometime during our lives. How do we cope when illness comes our way? How do we act and react when illness revises our plans and schedules? Strangely, there are some Christians who believe that we should never get sick. All sickness, they say, is due to either unconfessed sin or demonic possession. Agreed that, if we play fast and loose with our bodies, we may well reap what we sow and even dig our own grave, yet, according to the Bible, the possibility and actuality of sickness is just a fact of life in this fallen world - and Christians are not exempt from it.

Sick Christians

According to the Bible, Christians get sick too. Paul wrote reporting how *Trophimus I left ill at Miletus* (2 Timothy 4:19), and *Epaphroditus . . . was ill, near to death. But God had mercy on him . . .* (Philippians 2:27). And significantly, even the Apostle Paul himself - possibly the finest and most influential Christian who has ever lived - suffered at one time from an excruciating and debilitating *thorn in the flesh* (2 Corinthians 12:7), and benefited from the companionship and medical expertise of Luke, whom he described as *Luke, the beloved physician* (Colossians 4:14). Whilst Paul certainly would not have denied that Almighty God could heal us all instantly and miraculously if He saw fit, he also knew that God is under no obligation to do so. Paul also would have said that medicine and medical science - gifted doctors like Luke - are a blessing from God in this world of sickness, aches and pains.

Blessing from buffeting?

If we enjoy a busy and active life, being stopped in our tracks by illness can take some adjusting and adapting. Times of illness and enforced inactivity make us slow down. They also make us realise our frailty and humanity and that we are not indispensable, but totally dependant upon God and one another. We do not naturally welcome or desire sickness, but surely we can be thankful for it, if it has the effect of drawing us closer to our God and waiting upon Him. Psalm 119:67 reads *Before I was afflicted I went astray, but now I keep Thy Word.* Verse 71 of the same Psalm goes even further and testifies: *It is good for me that I was afflicted, that I might learn Thy statutes.*

The All-Embracing Providence of God

When we are forced to take to our home or a hospital bed, illness can seem to us like a terrible and pointless accident, ruining our perceived usefulness and fruitfulness in life. Perish such thoughts! Perish such thoughts because, if we believe the Bible, we are not allowed to believe in accidents, but only in divine *providence*. Providence is defined by the *Shorter Catechism* as 'God's most holy, wise and powerful preserving and governing all His creatures and all their actions.' We could state it more briefly though by saying that Providence means that 'absolutely everything ultimately comes from God.' *Are not two sparrows sold for a penny? And not one of them will fall to the ground without your Father's will* (Matthew 10:29). *For from Him and through Him and to Him are all things. To Him be glory for ever. Amen* (Romans 11:36).

In stating our belief in divine Providence, we have to be sensitive to the sufferings of others at the same time. Every Christian may have to confess at some time that 'God moves in a mysterious way, His wonders to perform.' As God is God, His ways have every right to be beyond His creatures on occasions. *The secret things belong to the LORD our God . . .* (Deuteronomy 29:29).

In Psalm 37:53 ff. we read that *The steps of a man are from the LORD . . . Though he fall, he shall not be cast headlong, for the LORD is the stay of his hand.* Thank God that He does indeed foreordain our steps. But thank God too that He has also foreordained our stops! In His Providence, He may see fit to give us a good, long, pain-free, sickness-free spell. But in His Providence, He may also see fit to lay us aside for either a short or a long period of time. This need not prevent us from praying to Him for health and healing and taking the appropriate medical measures: James 5:14 encourages us to pray for healing. But greater still, in both health and sickness - in both our steps and our stops - we may, with the Psalmist, know that the Lord is our stay and support. God's promise to every one of His children is: *I will never fail you nor forsake you* (Hebrews 13:5).

The best is yet to be!

Finally, take hope from that fact that, if we are Christians, we need never fear terminal illness, as, according to the Bible, there is no such thing. Christians are to live in the future tense! We have hope. One day, God is going to destroy all sickness and pain, and bring in His promised new heavens and new earth in which perfect righteousness and peace will dwell. This is referred to variously in the Bible as 'the kingdom of heaven' and 'eternal life.' We see a glorious foretaste of it in the ministry of Jesus when He came the first time. Sickness, sorrow, suffering, disease, demons and even death fled from all those to whom He ministered His saving grace. We, however, will not enjoy complete salvation - physical as well as spiritual, the redemption of the body as well as the soul - until the Lord Jesus comes again and gives us the new, spiritual (and pain and sickness free) bodies so wondrously described in various passages of the New Testament. The Old Testament however also looks forward with expectation to this most blessed of times. Isaiah described the coming kingdom of God thus: *And no inhabitant will say, 'I am sick'; the people who dwell there will be forgiven their iniquity* (Isaiah 33:24).

Afflicted Christian then, take heart. Seek God's grace to live with whatever He sends your way, and rejoice that in the New Jerusalem, all your sorrow and pain will be gone for ever.

O child of God wait patiently
When dark thy path may be
And let thy soul lean trustingly
On Him Who cares for thee
And though the clouds hang drearily
Upon the brow of night
Yet in the morning joy will come
And fill thy soul with light.

12

D.V.

A very godly Christian I once knew when I lived in Northern Ireland, used to pepper her conversation with the expression 'D.V.' We do not seem to hear the expression 'D.V.' very much today, but the initials stand for the Latin *Deo Volente* - which means 'God willing', or, more loosely, 'If the Lord wills'.

If we know our Bibles, we will know that 'D.V.' originates from a verse in the New Testament, namely James 4:15, which reads *If the Lord wills, we shall live and do this or that.*

If the Lord wills. . . The phrase reminds us that we are not in charge of our own destinies, but completely dependant upon God for all things. He is *the God in whose hand is your breath, and whose are all your ways* (Daniel 5:23). Timothy McVeigh, the Oklahoma bomber's last words before he went to the electric chair were: 'I am the master of my fate and the captain of my soul.' How wrong he was!

Who knows what awaits us in the days, weeks and months ahead? Only God does. We may have our hopes and plans, but they are subject to God's over all plan, whether we like it or not. *A man's mind plans his way, but the LORD directs his steps* (Proverbs 16:9). *A man's steps are ordered by the LORD; how then can man understand his way?* (Proverbs 20:24).

A joke amongst Jewish circles allegedly runs something like: Q. How do you make the Almighty laugh? A. Tell Him your plans. A Christian will certainly agree with the spirit of that joke, for we may propose, but God is perfectly entitled to dispose, for He is the God Who is over all, *Who accomplishes all things according to the counsel of His will* (Ephesians 1:11). Truth be told, if we could only remember that even our disappointments are His appointments, they would be a lot easier to bear.

'D.V.' Saying this is a recognition that all our lives are under God's control and subject to His will:-

> God holds the key of all unknown
> And I am glad
> If other hands should hold the key
> Or if He trusted it to me
> I might be sad
>
> I cannot read His future plans
> But this I know
> I have the smiling of His face
> And all the refuge of His grace
> While here below.

Every text has a context

If the Lord wills . . . It is a good motto to have and be gripped by. Let us read the verses before and after the phrase, so putting the verse into its context. James 4:13 ff. runs:-

Come now, you who say 'Today or tomorrow we will go into such and such a town and spend a year there and trade and get gain'; whereas you do not know about tomorrow. What is your life? For you are a mist that appears for a little time and then vanishes. Instead you ought to say, 'If the Lord wills, we shall live and do this or that.' As it is, you boast in your arrogance. All such boasting is evil.

The context of the verse is the uncertainly and fragility of life:- A man has great plans to go into a certain town and spend a year there and get rich in the process. He believes that his business idea is a sure fire winner. Such plans sound so sound, his friends assure him . . . But such plans do not account for the fact that Almighty God may take our ability to earn our own living away from us. It is his prerogative even to take away our very life. From a divine perspective, there is no such thing as a premature death. Our gifts, talents, health, wealth and life could be taken away right now if God sees fit. He may see fit to cut us down size, and give us a right sense of our own importance and His supreme importance. He alone is God!

Notice though that the context of our text includes the brevity of life as well as its fragility. *What is your life? For you are a mist that appears for a little time and then vanishes.* Life itself is brief and fragile. We British will never forget the death of Princess Diana. She was only in her thirties. Who would have thought that on that evening in Paris, when Princess Diana put on her expensive clothes and jewellery, and went out for an expensive meal with Dodi Al Fayad, that these would be her last moments on earth? All of our lives though, from the Princess to the pauper, are subject to the will of God. Saying 'D.V.' - *if the Lord wills* - acknowledges this fact. David confessed *I trust in Thee, O LORD, I say, 'Thou art my God.' My times are in Thy hand* (Psalm 31:14). The exact number of the days which we shall live on this earth has already been predetermined by Almighty God. *In Thy book were written, every one of them, the days that were formed for me, when as yet there was none of them* (Psalm 139:16).

Trust in the Lord

If the Lord wills. Our future hopes and plans are certainly subject to the will of God - *For from Him and through Him and to Him are all things* (Romans 11:36).

If we belong to the Lord Jesus though, we need not fear. Safely under our heavenly Father's loving sway, we are encouraged to trust His providence, and submit to whatever He sends our way, knowing that He is too wise to make mistakes, and too good to be unkind. Scripture affirms: *We know that in everything God works for good with those who love Him, who are called according to His purpose* (Romans 8:28) - and who are we to make ourselves the sole exception to this!

If the Lord wills. It is a good motto to remember and an anchor for our souls, for all of our plans are subject to the sovereign will of God.

All the way my Saviour leads me
What have I to ask beside?
Can I doubt His tender mercy
Who through life has been my guide?
Heavenly peace, divinest comfort
Here by faith in Him to dwell
For I know whate'er befall me
Jesus doeth all things well.

13

YOU REALLY ARE A SAINT!

It is not commonly known that, according to the Bible, every Christian is a saint. That every Christian is a saint may startle you, but, Biblically, it is the plain and sober truth - even though popular opinion would say that saints are an elite class of people who have attained a special sanctity which makes them eligible to be put (not literally!) into a stained glass window!

The word 'saint' means 'a holy one.' 'Holy', in this context means 'set apart for God' or sanctified by God. As every Christian has been set apart by God for God, it should comes as less of a surprise when we read Paul addressing the believers in ancient Corinth as 'saints.' Corinth was a city of vice. Humanly speaking, it was the most unholy place. Nothing that goes on today in our world would have shocked the residents of Corinth. Yet by the grace of God, Corinth had a church. Paul addressed this church as follows in his first letter to them:- *To the church of God which is at Corinth, to those sanctified in Christ Jesus, called to be saints together with those who in every place call on the name of our Lord Jesus Christ . . .* (1 Corinthians 1:2).

Every Christian then is a saint, and to explore this further we can consider this from three angles. There is the positional sense of being a saint; then there is the practical, progressive sense of being a saint, and then, in a coming day, there will be a time when every saint will be absolutely perfect.

1. Positional Sainthood

Every Christian is a saint, not intrinsically, but solely because of their relation to the Lord Jesus Christ. *We have been sanctified through the offering of the body of Jesus Christ once for all* (Hebrews 10:10). Those Corinthians, alluded to already, lived in a vile environment notorious for its immorality. What is more, at one time they partook of what this environment offered their lower instincts gladly and willingly. But God in Christ intervened, and saved them for Himself. After listing some of their former unholy 'activities', Paul then triumphantly went on to say *And such were some of you. But you were washed, you were sanctified, you were justified in the name of the Lord Jesus Christ and in the Spirit of our God* (1 Corinthians 6:11).

Every Christian is a saint by virtue of belonging to Jesus. Jesus lived a sinless life. Jesus died a sacrificial death for sinners. By faith, we partake of Him and He takes away our sin and clothes us with His perfect righteousness. The marvel is that God does not look at me as I am. He sees me 'in Christ' - washed in His blood, clothed with His righteousness and so for ever acceptable to a thrice holy God. Sainthood then is, first of all, positional. When we believe in Jesus we become a saint. This is a one off, never to be repeated event which, mercifully, can never be undone. Secondly though, and paradoxically, the New Testament also teaches that sainthood has a progressive, practical aspect to it as well - a growing up in Christ, if you like:-

2. Practical Sainthood

According to the Bible, a Christian is both a saint, and a Christian is called to be a saint - called to be holy, and called to live a life which pleases God. Certain things are incompatible with holiness, and so by God's grace and with the help of His Holy Spirit, we have to battle against them. So we read such verses as *Since we have these promises, beloved, let us cleanse ourselves from every defilement of body and spirit, and make holiness perfect in the fear of God* (2 Corinthians 7:1) and *Put to death what is earthly in you* (Colossians 3:5).

Christians then, paradoxically are both saints and are called to be saints. Our 'justification' is complete in Christ, but our 'sanctification' is a constant battle with us - a 'civil war' - an on-going process of 'ups and downs' which will never be perfect in this life. The *Shorter Catechism* defines sanctification this way:-

> Sanctification is the work of God's free grace, whereby we are renewed in the whole man after the image of God and are enabled more and more to die unto sin and to live unto righteousness.

The Christian which you see in this world therefore is not the finished product. We are in the making! As a car sticker once put it: 'Bear with me. God has not finished with me yet.'

So, every Christian is a saint. Every Christian is called to be a saint, and, finally, every Christian, by the grace of God, one day, will be a perfect saint. The process of sanctification will yet be completed:-

3. Perfect Sainthood

Hebrews 11:23 tells us that in God's heavenly city there are, right now, *the spirits of just men made perfect.* Perfection is unattainable in this life, for we are never free from our old nature. Sin will always indwell even the finest Christian in this life. The best of men are men at best.

In heaven though we will be forever free from sin, and thus fit to enjoy unblemished fellowship with God for all eternity. There, if we belong to Jesus, we will have the joy and privilege of taking our place among the saints who *have washed their robes and made them white in the blood of the Lamb. Therefore are they before the throne of God, and serve Him day and night within His temple* (Revelation 7:14,15).

Remember then that every Christian is a saint, and every Christian is called to be a saint, and every Christian will one day be a perfect saint. Nothing can hinder Almighty God from finishing and perfecting the work He has already begun in us. You're a saint!

I can think of no better way of closing this chapter on sainthood than by quoting Paul's prayer as follows:-

May the God of peace Himself sanctify you wholly; and may your spirit and soul and body be kept sound and blameless at the coming of our Lord Jesus Christ. He Who calls you is faithful, and He will do it (1 Thessalonians 5:23,24).

14

GOD'S POTS - OURSELVES!

In 1947, an Arab shepherd boy casually threw a stone into a cave by the shore of the Dead Sea. On investigating the sound of the shattered pottery that the stone made, he realised that the cave contained a collection of clay pots. Further investigation revealed that the pots contained ancient scrolls. These scrolls became known as the Dead Sea Scrolls. They were a priceless discovery, and they confirmed the accuracy of the text of the Bible. The complete scroll of the prophecy of Isaiah unearthed there at the Dead Sea is the oldest copy of the Scriptures in existence. No price can be put upon it. Talk about treasure in earthen pots!

Precious Treasure

In 2 Corinthians 4:7 Paul writes this about the treasure of the Gospel. *But we have this treasure in earthen vessels, to show that the transcendent power belongs to God and not to us.*

Precious Treasure in Earthen Vessels

The Gospel certainly is a priceless, precious treasure, for the Gospel is centred on *the precious blood of Christ* (1 Peter 1:19), shed for the forgiveness of sins at Calvary's cross. Saving faith in Christ enables us to possess personally the wonderful treasure of the Gospel of salvation. Faith enables us to possess Christ and all His benefits, and make them our own. Faith makes us rich with the eternal riches that cannot ever be taken away from us. Yet, says Paul, *we have this treasure in earthen vessels,* for the joys of salvation notwithstanding, we are still human and so subject to all the frailties of human nature - illness, injury, hurt, depression, disappointment and everything else which is part and parcel of 'life in the body.' It is only in the age to come, says Paul, that we will exchange these bodies of ours - earthen vessels - for something less fragile. Philippians 3:21 tells us that *the Lord Jesus Christ . . . will change our lowly body to be like His glorious body, by the power which enables Him even to subject all things to Himself.* At the moment though *we have this treasure in earthen vessels.* The picture highlights our weakness and frailty *to show that the transcendent power belongs to God and not to us.* We are weak, but He is mighty. He is the Creator, and we are His creatures. He is the King, and we are His subjects, totally dependant upon Him for everything, for *In Him we live and move and have our being* (Acts 17:28). Jesus told His disciples - and by implication, us - that *apart from Me you can do nothing* (John 15:5).

A Christian then, paradoxically, is a curious mixture of both the earthly and the heavenly, living in this world but with an eye to the next. Human, of course, yet an object of the grace of God in Jesus Christ - *vessels of mercy, which He has prepared beforehand for glory* (Romans 9:23).

Vessels of Salvation and Service

According to the Bible, vessels of salvation are also required to be vessels of service. The pots - ourselves - are not to be ornamental only, but they are to be used in God's service and purpose. The jars of the Dead Sea concealed their precious treasure for thousands of years. The Christian however is required to reveal and share the treasure of the Gospel. The Christian Faith is an evangelistic Faith. The Christian enjoys his spiritual treasures for sure, but he does not seek to hoard them. Rather he seeks to share them with all who will receive them too.

Utility Pots

In Paul's second letter to young Timothy, he takes up the imagery we are considering in this way:- *In a great house there are not only vessels of gold and silver but also of wood and earthenware, and some for noble use, some for ignoble. If any one purifies himself from what is ignoble, then he will be a vessel for noble use, consecrated and useful to the master of the house, ready for any good work* (2 Timothy 2:20,21). Oh then to be useable, useful and used by the Master! We may put ourselves at His disposal to be used - or laid aside - as He sees fit. We are required, says Paul, to do all that we can to be useable, that is, by His grace to purify ourselves and remove any impediments which may hinder our usefulness in God's service. Salvation always leads to service. Growing in service is part of the process of sanctification - 'the work of God's Spirit whereby we are renewed in the inner man after the image of God and are enabled more and more to die unto sin and to live unto righteousness' (*Shorter Catechism*).

Vessels of Mercy

A Christian may be described as 'a vessel of mercy.' We have treasure in an earthen vessel. God has chosen us and saved us, and He is shaping us for better things. He is the Potter, we are the clay. To get us into better shape may require pummelling, chiselling and painful moulding. It may even require a fiery trial in the oven of testing. But we can be sure that the all-wise, all-loving heavenly Potter knows what is best. He will surely fulfil His purpose for us, so that we will appear finally in His display room, not just as a vessel of mercy, but as a vessel of glory. *I am sure that He Who began a good work in you will bring it to completion at the day of Jesus Christ* (Philippians 1:6).

Treasure in earthen vessels . . . Every Christian should treat his fellow believers with care and respect. We are the objects of the blessing of Almighty God - yet we are also frail, and sometimes easily damaged. We are more dependant upon God and one another than perhaps we would readily admit. *Treasure in earthen vessels* - so HANDLE WITH SUPREME CARE!

15

REJECTION

Rejection

For this chapter, I should like us to consider the rather unpleasant topic of rejection. Under the word 'Reject', the dictionary includes the following:- 'put aside or discard as not to be accepted, used etc.' The definition though fails to capture the ghastly emotions which accompany being and feeling 'left out.' In my opinion, rejection ranks as one of the worst and most painful of all human experiences - yet we all have or will have experienced the unhappiness of rejection at some state in our lives. It is almost like a living bereavement. In schools you can witness unhappy children - those who somehow cannot blend in with the crowd and find friends. Then in adulthood, many of us know what it is to see others in active, fruitful employment, whilst we ourselves have been left out - consigned to the unemployed scrap heap, or under employed, grateful for a mundane job which at least gives us the dignity of being in work and not dependant on the state. Then there is the pain of rejection in the sphere of human relationships. Whilst many enjoy the love, warmth and support of family life, it mysteriously eludes others. Some apparently get 'left out' - excluded from being on the 'inside' of the blessing of human companionship. Rejection. Examples of it, from our own and others' experience could be multiplied.

The Rejected Saviour

When we turn to the Bible, we are struck by its down to earth nature. The Lord Jesus certainly understands any feelings of rejection which we have, as He Himself knew rejection and its accompanying feelings. Isaiah prophesied of Him: *He was despised and rejected by men; a man of sorrows and acquainted with grief* (Isaiah 53:3). John recorded of Him that : *He came to His own home, and His Own people received Him not* (John 1:11). It is good to remind ourselves then that none of our depths are ever deeper - and will ever be deeper - than the depths which our Saviour has already experienced. He knows what it is like to be human, sin apart. *We have not a high priest Who is unable to sympathise with our weaknesses ...* (Hebrews 4:15).

The Horror of Eternal Rejection

If rejection is awful in this life, and it is, imagine the horror of being eternally rejected by God - God, the source of all life, light and love. Actually, we lack the capacity to imagine the true reality of this. But think of what it would mean to be outside of God's blessing, and never having any part of it at all. Such a condition is hell indeed, and the Bible, very kindly, warns us of the existence of hell - a place to be shunned above all others. 2 Thessalonians 1:9 warns us of the eternal misery of hell for all those who reject God's Gospel of mercy in these words: *They shall suffer the punishment of eternal destruction and <u>exclusion</u> from the presence of the Lord and the glory of His might.* Here is an eternal rejection which will make the worst of earthly rejections seem pleasant by comparison. But the Bible was written so that this need not be the portion of any one:-

The Gospel of Acceptance for the Rejected

The Christian Gospel is Good News for the rejected. The bad news though precedes the Good, for the Bible is clear that by nature we are all excluded from God's presence because of our sin. It says *All we like sheep have gone astray . . .* (Isaiah 53:6), that is, we are out of God's flock. We are not in the warmth of His fold and under His tender, shepherd care.

The Gospel however proclaims that, in Christ, God rounds up the lost sheep and brings them into the warmth and safety of His fold. It is the Lord Jesus Who is the Good Shepherd Who rounds up His strays. He once told the following parable to illustrate His work: *'What man of you, having a hundred sheep, if he has lost one of them, does not leave the ninety nine in the wilderness, and go after the one which was lost, until he finds it? And when he has found it he lays it on his shoulders rejoicing. And when he comes home, he calls together his friends and his neighbours, saying to them, 'Rejoice with me, for I have found my sheep that was lost"* (Luke 15:4 ff.). A short time after, the Lord Jesus told the parable of the lost son. In this we read how the father of a wayward boy *saw him and had compassion, and ran and embraced him and kissed him* (Luke 15:20). Here we have a father's acceptance of his sinful, but repentant son. There followed a great and grand reconciliation. And the Gospel is the Gospel of reconciliation - it is God's embrace. The Gospel is the Gospel of God's acceptance of sinners in Christ and because of Christ.

Calvary: The Greatest Rejection of All

We have seen how Jesus knew rejection. Yet the rejection Jesus experienced was to reach its culmination and climax on the cross of Calvary. On the cross, Jesus was momentarily excluded from God's blessing that we might be eternally included. On the cross He bore our sins. This explains why when, on the cross, He cried out *'My God, my God, why hast Thou forsaken Me?'* (Matthew 27:46). A holy God can only reject sinners - unless there is a way for their sin to be pardoned. Such a way was found at Calvary, where Christ was rejected that we might be accepted. 2 Corinthians 5:21 - one of the most profound explanations of Calvary in the Bible - states: *For our sake He made Him to be sin Who knew no sin, so that in Him we might become the righteousness of God.* Hebrews 12:12 tells us that *Jesus also suffered outside the gate in order to sanctify the people through His Own blood.* Jesus suffered as an 'outsider' in every respect. He was, as it were, put out with the rubbish so that we might be gathered in with the jewels. He was put outside by men and by God, so that whoever believes in Him may know what it is to be 'inside'- inside of God's blessing for time and eternity.

Final Rejection or Final Acceptance

The very last chapter of the Bible - Revelation 22 - describes both eternal rejection and eternal acceptance. It tells of those either inside or outside the gates of the city of God - the glorious kingdom of heaven. If we are now outside the Christ Who suffered outside, we will be outside of that glorious place then, and for ever. If however, we are 'inside' the Christ Who suffered outside, whatever our lot in this life and whatever our experience of earthly rejection, on the authority of the Bible, we will enjoy the blessing of being eternally included. We will know the eternal love and acceptance of God in Christ for all eternity. Take heed. This is written for our warning. *Behold, now is the acceptable time; behold, now is the day of salvation* (2 Corinthians 6:2).

16

OUR UNCHANGING GOD

A favourite hymn of the English-speaking world includes the line 'Change and decay in all around I see.' Few would argue with the hymn writer here, for we live in a world characterised by change and decay - or as Paul put it *the creation was subject to futility . . . and bondage to decay* (Romans 8:20,21).

In our world of change and decay, Malachi 3:6 is a verse which is well worth memorising and being internally gripped by. The verse reads: '*For I the LORD do not change; therefore you, O sons of Jacob, are not consumed.*'

The Background

The brightness of the stars is revealed and appreciated most of all during the darkness of the night. Malachi prophesied during some very dark times of Israel's history. This being so, the verse here in Malachi 3:6 must have come to God's people as a bright star of promise during the night. How they must have appreciated its beam of light and hope.

We are always in danger of thinking that our times are unique, and that no times could be worse than our own, in a moral and spiritual sense. Malachi's day though seems to mirror our own in an uncanny way. From a reading of all four chapters of Malachi, we see that: - then as now, God was not generally honoured or feared; then as now, the divine worship that there was, was somewhat slipshod and lax; then as now, adultery, divorce, falsehood, oppression and cruelty were rife; then as now, religious apathy pervaded, and the law of heaven was exchanged for the lawlessness of hell, with the ensuing consequences for society at large. . .

Amidst the gloom, perplexity and uncertainty though, God Himself spoke. He spoke through His servant Malachi - a name that fittingly means 'my messenger.' God said to Israel then, and God says to us now: *'I the LORD do not change; therefore you, O sons of Jacob are not consumed.'* We are assured and reassured here of three great divine realities, namely: - 1. God's Constancy 2. God's Community and 3. God's Clemency.

1. God's Constancy

For I the LORD do not change . . . Such a statement is an encouragement to faith. In changing times we have an anchor for our souls in our unchanging God, the LORD our rock and our redeemer. He alone remains constant, faithful and dependable. He is *the Father of lights with Whom there is no variation or shadow due to change* (James 1:17). In changing times, we have an unchanging and an unchangeable God. And what is true of God the Father is as equally true of God the Son, for *Jesus Christ is the same yesterday and today and for ever* (Hebrews 13:8): -

> Yesterday, today forever
> Jesus is the same
> All may change, but Jesus never
> Glory to His name.

So whatever changes we may face, be they gradual or abrupt, we can rely on an unchanging God. Paul asks the rhetorical question *If God is for us, who is against us?* (Romans 8:31). The One Who is *for us* here is 'unchangeable in His being, wisdom, power, holiness, justice, goodness and truth' *(Shorter Catechism)*. This unchanging God has promised never to fail us or forsake us. This being so, we may face an uncertain future with confidence, and say:-

> Yesterday God helped me
> Today He'll do the same
> How long will this continue?
> Forever, praise His name.

Secondly though, we note that the star of promise in Malachi 3:6 also contains a reference to: -

2. God's Community

I the LORD do not change; therefore you, O sons of Jacob are not consumed. Note the *sons of Jacob.* The title refers to God's community. It shows that no matter how spiritually dark the era, God still has His people, even if they only seem a small, minority remnant. Even in Malachi's dark times, there were still those who genuinely belonged to the LORD and could testify to His saving grace. In Malachi 3:16 we read: *those who feared the LORD spoke with one another: the LORD heeded and heard them, and a book of remembrance was written before Him of those who feared the LORD and thought on His name.*

God Himself has seen to it and still sees to it that He has a community of His people here on earth. In a sense, His honour and glory depend on it. He had made a covenant with Abraham to be God to him and his descendants after him (Genesis 17:7). The *sons of Jacob,* redeemed by the blood of the lamb, were this covenant community. And God's Church today is the linear descendant of this community - they are the people of God on earth, redeemed by the blood of the Lamb. Galatians 3:29 reminds us *if you are Christ's then you are Abraham's offspring, heirs according to promise.*

Yes, the world around us may seem very dark and ungodly. Yet it cannot put out the light of God's saving grace. He will have a people for Himself - a redeemed company of people. Jesus said *'I will build My church, and the powers of death shall not prevail against it'* (Matthew 16:18). If you, through grace, are a member of this Church, then you have every reason to thank God and take courage.

Thirdly, we see that the bright star of promise in Malachi 3:6 also encourages us by drawing our attention to: -

3. God's Clemency

I the LORD do not change; therefore you, O sons of Jacob, are not consumed. Our verse reveals the clemency of the God of the Bible. Why did He not consume the sons of Jacob in His wrath? He had every right to do so. The answer lies solely in God's clemency. There is a clemency, a leniency, and a great mercy with Him. The same God had already revealed Himself to Moses in these words: *The LORD, the LORD, a God merciful and gracious, slow to anger and abounding in steadfast love and faithfulness* (Exodus 34:6). It is because of God's great mercy that none of us are consumed in His anger.

Living this side of Calvary and the empty tomb, we can claim to know more about God's clemency and mercy than Malachi ever knew. Malachi prophesied of the Messiah to come. In the Lord Jesus Christ his prophecy was fulfilled, and the Messiah arrived. In the Lord Jesus Christ, we can say that God's mercy became incarnate, for it is Jesus Who saves us from the wrath of God and makes the children of wrath the blessed children of God and heirs of glory. Such is the clemency of God. *In this is love, not that we loved God but that He loved us, and sent His Son to be the propitiation for our sins* (1 John 4:10).

Whilst ever there is time, God's mercy awaits the sinner and bestows the gift of saving faith in Jesus, the only Saviour of sinners. 2 Peter 3:9 tells us that *the Lord . . . is forbearing toward you, not wishing that any should perish but that all should reach repentance.* God's mercy spares us, even though it did not spare His beloved Son.

Thank God then for His unchanging promise in a changing world. It is still true: *I the LORD do not change, therefore you, O sons of Jacob are not consumed.* With God there is a dependable constancy, a delivered community and a divine clemency. If this God is our God, we need not fear. Knowing this God, we can step out into the future, taking the hand of Him Who is already there, for He says of Himself: *'I am the Alpha and the Omega' says the Lord God, Who is and Who was and Who is to come, the Almighty* (Revelation 1:8).

Before the hills in order stood
Or earth received her frame
From everlasting, Thou are God
To endless years the same

O God our help in ages past
Our hope for years to come
Be Thou our guard while life shall last
And our eternal home.

17

THE SHEPHERD AND HIS SHEEP

I will never forget the sight of a newly born lamb leaping. I saw this just as my teaching practice in West Wales was drawing to a close. They had posted me to a tiny town, where the sheep outnumbered the people! The 'powers that be', sent me there - one who had known nothing but city life - from January to March. When March came, Spring was just arriving, the flowers were just budding, and the ewes were just lambing, when . . . it was time for me to leave.

As the Bible was written in an eastern, agricultural setting, it is not surprising that sheep figure quite prominently in its pages. In Psalm 100, for instance - a Psalm of praise to God - the Psalmist likens God's relationship to His people as like that between a shepherd and his sheep. *Know that the LORD is God! It is He that made us, and we are His; we are His people and the sheep of His pasture* (Psalm 100:3). So let us explore this Biblical metaphor a little further:-

The Sheep's Straying and the Shepherd's Salvation

The picture of the shepherd and his sheep is employed by the

Bible to describe Christian salvation. By nature, it says, we are lost sheep - out of the fold and away from God's flock. *All we like sheep have gone astray; we have turned every one to his own way* (Isaiah 53:6).

The Christian Gospel proclaims the Good News that God in Christ came to rescue lost sheep like you and me. It is Christ Who rounds up lost sinners, and brings them into the safety of God's fold. Jesus once told a parable to this effect:-

'What man of you, having a hundred sheep, if he has lost one of them, does not leave the ninety-nine in the wilderness, and go after the one which is lost, until he finds it? And when he has found it, he lays it on his shoulders, rejoicing. And when he comes home, he calls together his friends and his neighbours, saying to them 'Rejoice with me, for I have found my sheep which was lost.' Just so, I tell you, there will be more joy in heaven over one sinner who repents than over ninety-nine righteous persons who need no repentance' (Luke 15:4-7).

The Sheep's Need and the Shepherd's Care

The picture of the shepherd and the sheep is used by the Bible to teach us that God not only saves us, but sustains us as well. In the famous Psalm - Psalm 23 - we have the well known words: *The LORD is my shepherd, I shall not want; He makes me lie down in green pastures. He leads me beside still waters* (Psalm 23:1,2).

Sufficient food, water and rest are basic requirements of sheep - and it is the shepherd's task to ensure that these requirements are met. In John 10:11, the Lord Jesus states: *'I am the Good Shepherd.'* As the Good Shepherd, you can be sure that His sheep will never be lacking in the necessary spiritual sustenance that is needed to sustain their spiritual life.

In Ezekiel 34, God asks the rhetorical question: *'Should not shepherds feed the sheep?'* (v.2). And then in vv. 12 ff., He goes on to promise: *'I (will) seek out My sheep . . . I will feed them on the mountain of Israel . . . I will feed them with good pasture, and upon the mountain heights of Israel shall be their pasture; there they shall lie down in good grazing land, and on fat pasture they shall feed on the mountains of Israel.*

I Myself will be the shepherd of My sheep, and I will make them lie down, says the Lord God.

A Christian is one who has been saved by God in Christ, and a Christian is one who is continually sustained and cared for by God in Christ. *We are His people and the sheep of His pasture.* Almighty God keeps a vigilant, shepherd's eye over His Own sheep, and ensures that we never lack anything essential for our true well being. Isaiah 40:11 says of God: *He will feed His flock like a shepherd, He will gather the lambs in His arms, He will carry them in His bosom.* It is picture language, of course. But the reality behind it is that of God's tender, unceasing, almighty care and concern for His people.

The Glory of the Shepherd and the Shepherd of the Glory

Lastly, let us take a peep into the eternal glory. Revelation 7 describes the redeemed in glory. But note verse 17. It says that *the Lamb in the midst of the throne will be their SHEPHERD, and He will guide them to springs of living water; and God will wipe away every tear from their eyes.*

A Christian therefore knows the shepherd-care of Christ, and a Christian will always know the shepherd-care of Christ - eternally. This Shepherd loves us with a love that will not let us go. Once in His sheepfold, we are eternally saved, safe and secure. The Bible definitely teaches the eternal security of the soul that has been saved by the Good Shepherd. Revelation 7 describes these, and Jesus definitely taught it, when He said *'My sheep hear my voice, and I know them, and they follow Me; and I give them eternal life, and they shall never perish, and no one shall snatch them out of My hand* (John 10:27.28).

This then begs the question: Do you know this Good Shepherd? Have you been saved by this Good Shepherd - the One Who laid down His life for the sheep (John 10:11)? Are you enjoying the sustenance of this Shepherd, Who feeds us daily by His Word of grace? Are you sure that, when you die, you will enjoy the company of the Good Shepherd for all eternity, and by His grace be eternally saved and eternally safe?

The King of love my Shepherd is
Whose goodness faileth never
I nothing lack, if I am His
And He is mine for ever.

18

'WHY DON'T YOU GROW DOWN!'

My two little nieces continue to further my education! It is always a joy to see them, but, as a 'thirty something' man, I cannot really be expected to be on the same wave-length as two eight and six year old girls. It is a happy arrangement though. As they are not my children, I can have fun with them, but I am absolved of all responsibility for them.

Did you know that the Lord Jesus Christ welcomed children? Did you know too that the Lord Jesus would have us, who are adults, to emulate children in certain respects? Consider carefully the following incident from Mark 10:13-16:-

And they were bringing children to Him, that He might touch them; and the disciples rebuked them. But when Jesus saw it He was indignant, and said to them 'Let the children come to Me, do not hinder them; for to such belongs the kingdom of God. Truly, I say to you, whoever does not receive the kingdom of God like a child shall not enter it.' And He took them in His arms and blessed them, laying His hands upon them.

I think, when I read that sweet story of old
When Jesus was here among men

How He called little children as lambs to His fold
I should like to have been with them then
I wish that His hands had been placed on my head
That His arms had been thrown around me
And that I might have seen His kind look when He said
'Let the little ones come unto Me!'

School teachers sometimes tell children to behave more like adults. But in this incident, the Lord Jesus is telling adults to behave more like children! What exactly did Jesus mean? I suggest the following:-

1. Children are characterised by a degree of openness and receptivity. It is when we get older that we get a bit more cynical and our minds become closed. This openness and receptivity, says Jesus, is also needed if we are to enter God's kingdom, for *'whoever does not receive the kingdom of God like a child shall not enter it.'* It reminds us that salvation is a gift to receive by faith, not a reward to achieve by our own merits. *For by grace you have been saved through faith; and this is not your own doing, it is the gift of God - not because of works, lest any man should boast* (Ephesians 2:8,9).

2. Children are characterised by dependence. They are not self- sufficient. They are actually quite helpless, and rely totally on the love, wisdom and provision of their parents and others. As yet, their abilities are dormant and undeveloped. They have no economic power and so are dependent on their parents, or teachers or nurses.
We who are adults though are actually totally dependent as well. We are totally dependent on God - more than we ever realise. We do not deserve anything from Him, and yet He provides for us, and meets our every physical and spiritual need. 'I need Thee every hour' says the hymn. And so we do. *In Him we live and move and have our being* (Acts 17:28). He is *the God in Whose hand is your breath* (Daniel 6:23).

3. Children are naturally curious and inquisitive - like a blank sheet of paper, ready to be written on.

We too should be open to God's Word. The Bible is God's Word written, therefore our greatest longing should be to know it, understand it and obey it - as well as grapple with it and pray and ponder over it and consider how it applies to us and our particular, individual situations. *Open my eyes, that I may behold wondrous things out of Thy law* (Psalm 119:18). *Teach me, O LORD, the way of Thy statutes; and I will keep it to the end* (Psalm 119:33). God promises the blessed illumination of His Holy Spirit to all those who ask Him, to help them understand the Bible.

4. Children are under authority. Parents are in charge. Children rebel against this authority to their own detriment. This reminds us that in calling God our 'Father', we are employing a word which denotes authority as well as affection. Our Father is God - the Sovereign of the universe. He is *the Most High. His dominion is an everlasting dominion, and His kingdom endures from generation to generation* (Daniel 4:34).

> The Lord is King! Who then shall dare
> Resist His will, distrust His care
> Or murmur at His wise decrees
> Or doubt His royal promises?

People rebel against the Lord Jesus at their own peril. He will have His way, for He is the *King of kings and Lord of lords* (Revelation 19:16). There is no higher authority than His, hence Psalm 2:11,12: *Serve the LORD with fear, and rejoice with trembling. Kiss the Son, lest He be angry, and ye perish from the way, when His wrath is kindled but a little. Blessed are all they that put their trust in Him* (KJV).

5. Children instinctively run to their parents when they are in distress. We who are Christians have a similar resource. We have the avenue of prayer. Prayer, as it were 'taps us in' to our Father in heaven, our sympathetic Saviour and the blessed help and comfort of the Holy Spirit. We have a God to Whom we can turn and pour out all our burdens. He says *Call on Me in the day of trouble; I will deliver you, and you shall glorify Me* (Psalm 50:15).

6. Lastly, children accept their station in life. They are children and not adults. They enjoy much but understand relatively little, receiving much by love and through unquestioning trust.

Oh to be able to accept the lot God has allotted to us in life too! When the apostle Peter asked the Lord about His plans for John, Jesus replied *'What is that to you? Follow Me!'* (John 21:22). He says the same to us when we are tempted to think that God's will for others is somehow more rosier than His will for ourselves.

Whilst we are obliged to change certain aspects of our characters - we are commanded to mortify our sinful tendencies - there is much in us that we cannot change without going against the grain. God has made us as we are. You are the only you. You are unique. Happiness results from accepting the way God has made us, and walking the path which He has set down before us, and keeping our eyes on Him and not upon others.

> Have Thine Own way Lord
> Have Thine Own Way
> Thou art the Potter
> I am the clay
> Mould me and make me
> After Thy will
> While I am waiting
> Yielded and still.

Children then do not know a lot, yet surprisingly, they can teach us a great deal, especially in the spiritual realm. Remember the words of the Lord Jesus Christ: *to such* (that is, children) *belongs the kingdom of God. Truly, I say to you, whoever does not receive the kingdom of God like a child shall not enter it.*

This all being so, we should really pray 'Lord, give me child-like faith in you.'

19

THE MOTHER SIDE OF GOD THE FATHER

I have headed this chapter with the rather provocative title of 'The mother side of God the Father'. It may seem to you to be a contradiction in terms, but read on to find out more:-

God the Father

It almost goes without saying that the designation given to the God of the Bible is invariably a male designation. Those so called 'feminist theologians' who distort the Bible otherwise are best given a wide berth. Psalm 103:13, for instance, reads *As a father pities his children, so the LORD pities those who fear Him.* The Lord Jesus Christ likewise taught His followers to pray the famous prayer which begins by addressing God as *Our Father Who art in heaven* (Matthew 6:9).

One of the primary Christian blessings is that of 'adoption', that is, being brought, by God's grace in Christ, into the family of God, with all its ensuing blessings, benefits and privileges. Only when, by God's grace, we have been brought into His family, can we truly know and call God 'Father'. Thus, in Galatians 4:6, Paul writes to Christians explaining the fact that *because you are sons, God has sent the Spirit of His Son into our hearts, crying, 'Abba! Father!'* Knowing God as Father then is a Christian basic. Addressing God as Father speaks volumes of His love and grace and our dependence upon Him, as well as His authority over us as we live out our lives - He may see fit to subject us to His loving fatherly discipline, especially if we go astray.

God's Fatherhood then, and our corresponding sonship is a most blessed doctrine and fact of Christian experience - as every truly born-again believer can testify.

God the Mother?

Did you know though that the Bible reveals that there is also a mother side to God the Father? Consider these verses from Isaiah 49:14-16:-

But Zion said, 'The LORD has forsaken me, my Lord has forgotten me.' 'Can a woman forget her sucking child, that she should have no compassion on the son of her womb? Even these may forget, yet I will not forget you. Behold, I have graven you on the palms of My hands; your walls are continually before Me.'

The verses here ask a question. They speculate: Can, or would, a mother forget about her helpless baby? Our answer would no doubt be that it is doubtful, even inconceivable, that she ever would. The bond between a mother and her baby is surely one of the strongest of human ties. Yet saying this, we know that the horror of a mother abandoning her baby is not unknown in this fallen world. News headlines have informed us of children who have died from neglect. But in these verses, God assures - and reassures - His people, that He will never forsake them. The worst possible scenario in the physical world - a mother forgetting her baby - will not happen in the spiritual realm. God says: *'I will not forget you. Behold, I have graven you on the palms of My hands.'* Similarly, in the New Testament we read God's promise: *'I will never fail you nor forsake you'* (Hebrews 13:5), and Romans 8:39 assures us that absolutely nothing *in all creation will be able to separate us from the love of God in Christ Jesus our Lord.*

He cares about you

Just as a child is dependent upon its mother for much, how much more reason have God's children to depend on Him and trust Him for all things, knowing that He will not cast us off or out, and knowing that He is committed to our earthly and eternal welfare. His love is a loyal love. His love is a covenant love which promises 'I will be your God, and you will be My people.'

The mother side of God the Father is, admittedly, not as high profile in the Scriptures as His Father side. But the fact that it is there at all can be of immense comfort to God's children. It was perhaps with Isaiah's verses in mind that the hymn writer wrote the following. Putting words into God's mouth, he writes:-

> Can a mother's tender care
> Cease towards the babe she bare?
> Yes, she may forgetful be
> Yet I will remember thee
>
> Mine is an unchanging love
> Higher than the heights above
> Deeper than the depths beneath
> Free and faithful, strong as death.

The Tender Christ

What though, when we come to the fullness of time, and consider the Lord Jesus Christ in relation to our chapter heading concerning God's 'motherhood'? The Lord Jesus is the unsurpassed revelation of God, for He is God in the flesh. Jesus, of course, was male - He is the Son of God and God the Son. Yet Scripture reveals that even Jesus had a feminine, motherly facet to His character. When He expressed His intense concern over the city of Jerusalem, He described Himself as a loving, protective mother hen:- *'How often would I have gathered your children together as a hen gathers her brood under her wings'* (Matthew 23:37). It reminds us that we may flee to Jesus for safety and protection - just as a child instinctively flees to its mother when it is hurt or troubled.

The Apostle Paul

Finally, consider the apostle Paul. A more manly, muscular and godly Christian could not be envisaged than Paul. But even he - reflecting something of the divine character - had a mother side to him. We evidence this from what we know of his dealings with the Christians in Thessalonica. Writing to them, he reported how *we were gentle among you, like a nurse taking care of her children* (1 Thessalonians 2:7).

Wanted: Christian Mothers

Growing into the people that God wants us to be then, should make us - even we men - become more like a good mother. God's tender side reveals a mother side to Him, as we have seen, and grace will make us reflect this.

When the world is full of damaged, hurting people, bearing an unwritten FRAGILE: HANDLE WITH CARE, perhaps we would all do well to consider more the mother side of God the Father as revealed in the Bible - and by His grace seek to become more like Him, for the blessing of souls and the glory of His name.

20

HOPE FOR THE SORELY TROUBLED

Some less well known verses of Scripture read like this:-

Thou Who hast made me see many sore troubles wilt revive me again; from the depths of the earth Thou will bring me up again. Thou wilt increase my honour, and comfort me again (Psalm 71:20,21).

The verses are not widely known, but what a blessing they are when we know them - especially when we, like the Psalmist, also find ourselves experiencing *sore troubles*.

Christ in all the Scriptures

In the Bible, all roads lead to Christ, the Word of God in the flesh. The verses here are no exception, for they can be applied to Him.

God made His Own Son to see *sore troubles* for sure. No more was this so than when He died on the cross. 2 Corinthians 5:21 says that at the cross, God made Christ actually *to be sin*, that is, to be accounted liable for the punishment for sins not His Own. It was all for the purpose of procuring the eternal salvation of God's people. Christ was sorely troubled so that whoever believes in Him may be surely saved.

The death of Christ on the cross though was not the end of the story. *Thou wilt bring me up again. Thou wilt increase my honour, and comfort me again.* After Christ's loving and careful burial in Joseph's tomb, God raised His Son to life again. Christianity is founded on the resurrection of Christ from the grave. Forty days later, Christ ascended gloriously into heaven and since then has been seated at the right hand of God, in His place of rightful and unrivalled pre-eminence. *God has highly exalted Him and bestowed on Him the name which is above every name* (Philippians 2:9).

So the verses from Psalm 71 give us a glimpse of Christ - Christ in His death, resurrection and glorification. Yet the verses can also be applied to ourselves equally well:-

A Christian's Troubles

Thou Who hast made me see many sore troubles . . . Realism tells us that we can expect to suffer in this life. Suffering is one of the consequences of living in a fallen world. When sin entered the world, the harmony of the world went, and the world went somewhat out of synchronisation. As if we did not know! Suffering is a consequence of sin - ill health, family tensions, trouble and tension at work, redundancy, unemployment, violence, wars between nations . . . they are inevitable. The verse though may shock some in that it says that ultimately, looking beyond 'secondary causes' it is God Himself Who sends sore troubles our way, for reasons best known to Himself.

Be forewarned then. Expect *sore troubles.* No one is exempt from them. Troubles of various kinds are sure to come to you - troubles which bring you to an end of yourself and cast you much more closely on God for support. Sore troubles are surely sore, but they are not the full picture, for the verses are equally concerned with:-

A Christian's Triumph

Thou . . . wilt revive me again; from the depths of the earth Thou wilt bring me up again. Thou wilt increase my honour, and comfort me again.

In this life then, no one need be written off totally. There is always hope for us whilst ever we are looking to God. The Psalmist's focus is most definitely God-ward. In this we are given an example to emulate. Look to God then! None of our depths are too deep for Him. None of our difficulties are too great for Him and none of our trials are too severe for His promised all-sufficient grace. Hence we can say: *Rejoice not over me, O my enemy; when I fall, I shall rise; when I sit in darkness, the LORD will be a light to me* (Micah 7:8).

> Got any rivers you think are uncrossable?
> Got any mountains you can't tunnel through?
> God specializes in things thought impossible
> And He can do what no other pow'r can do.

Paul's pains

The Apostle Paul - one of the finest Christian ambassadors ever - also knew *sore troubles*. If he was not exempt, as neither was the Saviour Himself, who are we to expect a trouble-free ride to heaven? Paul knew his troubles - yet Paul also knew God's deliverance, help and all-sufficient grace. Every Christian may know the same too, for God is no respecter of persons. Take hope then from Paul's testimony as given. He knew his afflictions, yet equally he knew God's deliverance. Consider well Paul's hard experience, as related in 2 Corinthians 1:8 ff. :-

For we do not want you to be ignorant, brethren, of the affliction we experienced in Asia; for we were so utterly, unbearably crushed that we despaired of life itself. Why, we felt that we had received the sentence of death; but that was to make us rely not on ourselves but on God Who raises the dead; He delivered us from so deadly a peril, and He will deliver us; on Him we have set our hope that He will deliver us again.

Better days are ahead!

It is so easy to become locked into the present, but present trials are not the whole story. Looking to the God and Father of our Lord

Jesus Christ, there is always hope. We need never despair. Our verses end with the affirmation: *Thou wilt increase my honour and comfort me again.* While we cannot rule out applying this to this life, it surely, ultimately refers to heaven. For in heaven all of our sorrows, trials, pains, perplexities and *sore troubles* will be over - gone for ever and never to return. *God will wipe away every tear from their eyes* (Revelation 7:17).

> There's no disappointment in heaven
> No weariness, sorrow or pain
> No hearts that are bleeding and broken
> No song with a minor refrain
> The clouds of our earthly horizon
> Will never appear in the sky
> For all will be sunshine and gladness
> With never a sob or a sigh.

Take heart then troubled Christian. God is on your side! Repeat Psalm 71:20,21 over and over again. By faith say: *Thou Who hast made me see many sore troubles wilt revive me again; from the depths of the earth Thou wilt bring me up again. Thou wilt increase my honour and comfort me again.*

21

BETHANY - JESUS' HOME FROM HOME

We have seen in a previous chapter that the Lord Jesus was no stranger to the pain of rejection. *He was despised and rejected by men* (Isaiah 53:3). *He came to His Own home and His Own people received Him not* (John 1:11). Whilst this was true, there was yet one place where Jesus was always made welcome. He was always welcome at the home or Martha, Mary and Lazarus, two sisters and one brother who lived in Bethany. Bethany is a village two miles outside of Jerusalem, situated on the Mount of Olives.

For this chapter, let us go to Bethany. Bethany was a welcome respite for the Lord Jesus. There, in that home, He enjoyed warm friendship and welcome relief from the labours of His ministry and the onslaughts of His enemies. In our mind's eye, let us pay a brief visit to Bethany now - a place, for the Christian, forever hallowed by its association with the Lord Jesus Christ:-

1. Bethany : A Place of Priorities

Bethany was a place of priorities. In Martha and Mary's home, Luke records how *Mary . . . sat at the Lord's feet and listened to His teaching* (Luke 10:39). For doing this, she was commended by the Lord. He said *'One thing is needful. Mary has chosen the good portion, which shall not be taken away from her'* (Luke 10:42).

There is a lesson for Christians in the 21st century here, and it is this: do not neglect the 'one thing that is needful.' Be careful to guard - to jealously guard - a time of fellowship with Jesus every day. Ensure that the fires of devotion stay fuelled. Take time to listen to the Lord Jesus. Take time to speak to Him. Take time to enjoy His presence. There are so many distractions around us, connected with our work and our leisure. Good and necessary things - as well as unnecessary and illegitimate things - can hinder our fellowship with Christ. Don't let the good rob you of the best. It has been well said that if we are too busy for prayer and reading God's Word, then we really are too busy.

> Take time to be holy, speak oft with thy Lord
> Abide in Him always, and feed on His Word
> Make friends of God's children, help those who are weak
> Forgetting in nothing His blessing to seek
>
> Take time to be holy, the world rushes on
> Spend much time in secret with Jesus alone
> By looking to Jesus like Him thou shalt be
> Thy friends, in thy conduct, His likeness shall see.

2. Bethany : A Place of Power

Bethany was a place of power - divine power. That special home in Bethany was not exempt from sorrow, for Mary and Martha knew what it was to lose their brother Lazarus. At one time, Lazarus died, leaving the sisters grief stricken. But John 11 relates how the Lord Jesus - demonstrating the omnipotent power of God Himself - actually raised Lazarus back to full life and health. Lazarus had been dead and buried for four days, but John records the staggering miracle of how Jesus went to his tomb and *cried with a loud voice 'Lazarus come out.'* And then *The dead man came out, his hands and feet*

*bound with bandages, and his face wrapped with a cloth. Jesus said to them,
'Unbind him, and let him go'* (John 11:43,44).

The incident is quite outstanding. Yet it is so in-line with John's
Gospel - a Gospel which demonstrates clearly the deity of Christ
and His unique ability to bestow eternal life on all who believe in
Him. *These are written that you may believe that Jesus is the Christ, the
Son of God, and that believing you may have life in His name* (John 20:31).

Moments before Jesus raised Lazarus from death, He made this
great claim for Himself in John 11:25,26: *'I am the resurrection and the
life; he who believes in Me, though he die, yet shall he live, and whoever
lives and believes in Me shall never die.* Jesus' raising of Lazarus back
to life again confirmed the truth of this staggering claim completely.
Jesus alone can give new life - the forgiveness of sins, peace with
God, a home in heaven, and eventually a new, resurrected body,
suitable for the new heavens and new earth promised by God in
His Own time.

3. Bethany : A Place of Perfume

Bethany was a place of perfume. John 12 describes a most touch-
ing incident which occurred there:-

Jesus' death on the cross was just a week away. He knew all too
well what lay before Him, for it was for this that He had left heaven
for earth. But now there was a brief peace before the storm, as Jesus
was in Bethany, enjoying supper with Martha, Mary and Lazarus.
John 12:3 describes how, on this occasion *Mary took a pound of costly
ointment of pure nard and anointed the feet of Jesus and wiped His feet
with her hair; and the house was filled with the fragrance of the ointment.*

Bethany then, was a place of perfume - the perfume of Mary's
devotion to the Lord Jesus. In the Bible, devotion to God is often
described in fragrant terms: *Let my prayer be counted as incense before
Thee* (Psalm 141:2). *Noah built an altar to the LORD . . . And offered
burnt offerings on the altar. And . . . the LORD smelled the pleasing odour*
(Genesis 8:20). Mary's anointing of the Lord Jesus here in Bethany
evidences her sincere and costly devotion to her Lord. Her action
also betrayed great understanding too:-

Mary's anointing of Jesus showed that she recognised Him as the longed for Messiah - the word 'Messiah' means 'anointed one.' But her anointing of Jesus also showed that she realised the vital importance of the death of Jesus in the divine plan and scheme. *'She has anointed My body beforehand for burying'* (Mark 14:8). Paradoxically, it is in the death of Jesus that we find life. It is by His cross that we may escape the condemnation we deserve for our sins. It is by the sacrifice of His sinless life, that we, sinners though we are, may receive God's eternal salvation.

Mary understood the necessity of Christ's death. Many did not see it in Jesus' day. The cross was a stumbling block then, as it is now, and always will be to those outside of Christ - to those who seek to weave their own salvation by what they do and who they are, and thus have no place for the cross of Calvary in their thinking. *For the word of the cross is folly to those who are perishing, but to us who are being saved it is the power of God* (1 Corinthians 1:18).

So what a delightful place was Bethany. In Bethany Jesus enjoyed a home from home. It was a place of priorities - where Mary listened attentively to Jesus' teaching. It was a place of power - where Jesus raised Lazarus from the dead and it was a place of perfume - where Mary anointed Jesus for burial, and the fragrance of her devotion filled the house.

All the above being so, oh that our hearts, homes and churches had more of the 'Bethany spirit' about them - that is, that they are places where the Lord Jesus Christ Himself is known and enjoyed as an unseen, yet very real and Special Guest.

22

'LOOK AT THE BIRDS OF THE AIR'

A minister friend of mine is a keen bird watcher. The technical term for this is ornithology - though bird watchers sometimes refer to themselves as 'twitchers'. That aside, each morning sees my friend and his wife having their breakfast in front of the bay window which overlooks their back   garden. The bird table, strategically placed there attracts all sorts of birds, all the year around, and they take great delight in spotting and categorising them.

In Matthew 6:26, the Lord Jesus tells us to: '*Look at the birds of the air . . .*' In this chapter, I should like us to heed the Lord's injunction here. Let us look at some of the birds of the Bible, and see what they have to teach us.

1. The Birds of Salvation

In Exodus 19:4, God says to the people of Israel: '*You have seen what I did to the Egyptians, and how I bore you on eagles' wings and brought you to Myself.*' We have here the birds of salvation.

The Israelites were in slavery in Egypt. It was cruel and heartless - but God in His mercy intervened. He redeemed them. He delivered them from their slavery and entered into a close, covenant relationship with them. He brought them to Himself - and there can be no greater blessing than that. The Exodus from Egypt is central to the Old Testament. It really happened, but from our New Testament perspective we can see in it a picture of the greater salvation accomplished by Christ. Jesus delivers us from the penalty and power of sin. Jesus enables us to soar above the condemnation we really deserve, and Jesus will yet enable us to 'soar on eagles' wings' when we leave this world, and ascend to the home in heaven which He is currently preparing for us. Thank God then for the birds of salvation.

2. The Birds of Succour

In Matthew 6:26, Jesus says *'Look at the birds of the air: they neither sow nor reap nor gather into barns, and yet your heavenly Father feeds them. Are not you of more value than they?'* Here we observe the birds of succour and support. They encourage us to trust God to provide for all our needs. Here, Jesus reasons from the lesser to the greater. If God cares for a little bird, He says, how much more will He care and provide for one made in His image and redeemed by the blood of His Own Son. Philippians 4:19 corroborates this thought when it states *And my God will supply every need of yours according to His riches in glory in Christ Jesus.* The birds of the air then are a reminder that we are to trust in God. He is infinitely worthy of our trust, and will never let us down.

> Said the Robin to the Sparrow
> 'I would really like to know
> Why these anxious human beings
> Rush around and worry so?'
>
> Said the sparrow to the Robin
> 'Friend, I think that it must be
> That they have no heavenly Father
> Such as cares for you and me.'

3. The Birds of Sovereignty

In Matthew 10:29, Jesus says: *'Are not two sparrows sold for a penny? And not one of them will fall to the ground without your Father's will?'* We have here the birds of sovereignty - or more specifically, the birds of divine sovereignty.

The 'sparrow of God's sovereignty' is a welcome reminder that our God reigns. He is on the throne. It is He Who is in charge and final control of this, at times, very perplexing world. Every major and minor happening is due not to accident or 'fate', but to God's all-wise and all-embracing will. The *Shorter Catechism* defines God's works of providence as 'His most holy, wise and powerful preserving and governing all His creatures and all their actions.' His providence extends to the movement of vast planets, and His providence extends to the death of a little, nameless sparrow. Again, apply the logic of Jesus' words: If a little sparrow's life is ruled and over-ruled by God, how much more the lives of His Own children - you and me. Romans 8:28: *We know that in everything God works for good with those who love Him, who are called according to His purpose.*

4. The Birds of Security

The birds of the air also teach us about security. Psalm 36:7 reads: *How precious is Thy steadfast love, O God! The children of men take refuge in the shadow of Thy wings.* 'The shadow of Thy wings' is a common Old Testament expression. It is - as we saw in a previous chapter - picture language, for *God is spirit'* (John 4:24) and thus has no literal wings. The teaching behind the language though is this: Just as a frightened baby bird takes refuge under the shadow of its mother's wing, so God's children may, figuratively speaking, take refuge under His almighty wing. There is no safer place in all the world. No natural or supernatural force can harm us 'in the shadow of Thy wings.' *The LORD is my rock and my fortress and my deliverer, my God, my rock in Whom I take refuge, my shield, and the horn of my salvation, my stronghold* (Psalm 18:2). *Under His wings you will find refuge* (Psalm 91:4).

As an interesting and amazing aside, we note that in Matthew 23:37, the Lord Jesus said this of Jerusalem: *'How often would I have gathered your children together as a hen gathers her brood under her wings.'* We have here one of the less well known evidences of Jesus' deity, for here He takes an Old Testament picture of God and applies it to Himself. Such audacity would be totally blasphemous, were it not actually true.

Lastly though, in our 'Bible bird watch', we note some rather formidable birds:-

5. The Birds of Sorrow

In horrific language, Revelation 19 describes the birds of the air feeding on the dead bodies of the enemies of God. It is not pleasant reading, but the message of the Bible here and elsewhere is clear: God will be victorious and will conquer all those who are opposed to Him, and consign them to eternal punishment. This being so, it is incumbent upon us to ensure that we are actually on God's side. This in turn begs the crucial question: Do we belong to Jesus? Has Jesus dealt with the enmity that separates us and God? Have we truly been reconciled to God by the death of Christ on the cross?

'Look at the birds of the air' said the Lord Jesus. We have. We have looked at some Bible birds - birds which speak of God's salvation, God's provision, God's sovereignty, God's protection and God's ultimate victory over all His enemies. May these birds truly be our teachers. And if we are Christians, let us rejoice that, if God cares for the little birds, how much more has He cared, does He care and will He care for you and me.

There is a hymn which is suitable for God's children of all ages. It goes like this:-

God Who made the earth
The air the sky the sea
Who gave the light its birth
Careth for me

God Who sent His Son
To die on Calvary
He if I lean on Him
Will care for me

When in heaven's bright land
I all His loved ones see
I'll sing with that blest band
'God cared for me.'

23

EN GEDI - THE OASIS IN THE WILDERNESS

1 Samuel 23:29 informs us that when David was fleeing from King Saul's evil intentions on his life, *he (David) went . . . and dwelt in the strongholds of En-gedi.*

En-gedi is a beautiful oasis half way along the Israeli shore of the Dead Sea. Its name means 'fountain/spring of a kid', and its springs, waterfalls, lush vegetation and greenery stand out in stark contrast to the arid, desert wilderness round about it. The date palms at En-gedi are a sight to behold. It is just amazing the difference fresh water makes.

Let us, for this chapter, pay a little visit to En-gedi. May the spiritual lessons of that beautiful spot be a spiritual oasis now to us in the desert wilderness of this secular world:-

1. Song of Solomon 1:14 reads: *My beloved is to me a cluster of henna blossoms in the vineyards of En-gedi.* En-gedi, as I have mentioned, has a constant supply of fresh water all year around. It is this which makes it so different from the general deadness of the Dead Sea and the desert wilderness which surrounds it.

Spiritually, we have to say that this world is characterised by deadness. 'Change and decay in all around I see' says the hymn. Yet when we know the Lord Jesus, we have an oasis of life, in this world and the next. Jesus promises living water to all who believe in Him. John 7:37 ff. reads: *Jesus stood up and proclaimed, 'If any one thirst, let him come to Me and drink. He who believes in Me, as the Scripture has said, 'Out of his heart shall flow rivers of living water."*

As En-gedi is an oasis of life amidst death, so it is Jesus Who is the giver of eternal life, just as it is Jesus Who enables us to live a fruitful life to the glory of God.

2. En-gedi was a place of refuge and safety. It has many caves, and it was in one of these that David hid when he was fleeing for his life from King Saul.

i. Eternal Safety

In the Lord Jesus too, the believer has a place of safety and refuge. Jesus is the One Who delivers us from the most fearful and ultimate danger of all, namely the wrath of God against sin. *Jesus . . . delivers us from the wrath to come* (1 Thessalonians 1:10).

It is the cross of Christ and the Christ on the cross which alone brings eternal safety - deliverance from the penalty of sin and deliverance from an eternity in hell. In Jesus then we have eternal safety. As soon as we are enabled to pray the sinner's initial prayer - 'Rock of Ages, cleft for me, let me hide myself in Thee'- then our souls are eternally saved and eternally safe.

ii. Earthly Refuge

But where do we go for refuge in our earthly troubles? *Man is born to trouble as the sparks fly upward* (Job 5:7). None of us are exempt from pain and perplexity in this life. Difficulties come our way, as do losses and crosses, stresses and distresses. Where do we go when we are hurting and troubled? Is there an oasis for us - an En-gedi amidst the heat? Yes there is!

The Christian life not only commences by seeking refuge in God, but it continues by seeking and finding refuge in God as well - and will do so until we enjoy eternal refuge and safety by the *springs of living water* (Revelation 7:17) when this life is over.

The Christian has the inestimable privilege of enjoying refuge in a Person, not a place - safety in none less than God Himself. Think about the following Scriptures:-

Nahum 1:7: *The LORD is good, a stronghold in the day of trouble; He knows those who take refuge in Him.*

Then there is Psalm 57 - a Psalm actually written by David 'on location' at En-gedi, whilst fleeing from Saul. It is a Psalm which we can make our own whenever the troubles we do not desire nevertheless come our way. The Psalm opens like this:-

Be merciful to me, O God, be merciful to me, for in Thee my soul takes refuge; in the shadow of Thy wings I will take refuge, till the storms of destruction pass by. I cry to God Most High, to God Who fulfils His purpose for me. He will put to shame those who trample upon me. God will send forth His steadfast love and faithfulness . . .

En-gedi. It is a place of life amidst death; a place of fruitfulness amidst barrenness, and a place of safety amidst danger. God in Christ is all these and more to the believing soul. In Jesus we may enjoy a spiritual oasis amidst the barrenness of this world. In Jesus we have eternal and earthly refuge, safety and salvation. How vital it is therefore that we flee to the spiritual oasis which is the Lord Jesus Christ.

Charles Wesley composed the following. It sums up much of what we have considered about the spiritual lessons of the oasis of En-gedi:-

> Thou hidden source of calm repose
> Thou all-sufficient love divine
> My help and refuge from my foes
> Secure I am, if Thou art mine
> And lo! From sin and grief and shame
> I hide me, Jesus, in Thy Name

In want my plentiful supply
In weakness my almighty power
In bonds my perfect liberty
My light in Satan's darkest hour
My help and stay whene'er I call
My life in death, my heaven, my all.

24

SALT

Question. What does not taste very nice on its own, but makes other foods taste nicer? When I asked this question during a Sunday School lesson once, almost every hand shot up, and a wee girl on the front row gave me the right answer first time. 'Salt!' Salt was the answer I was looking for. Salt does not taste very nice on its own, yet it enhances the flavour of many foods. If fact, without salt, many foods can be a bit flavourless and insipid.

If you know the Bible, you will know that it often takes up ordinary, everyday objects and uses them to teach us extraordinary lessons. It takes up the things of earth and uses them to teach us about the truth of heaven. And this is so with common or garden salt - that substance we use everyday, almost unthinkingly. So what does the Bible have to say about salt?

1. The Salt of the Covenant

'Covenant' is a great Bible word. So central is it to the Book, that the Bible is actually divided into the old and new covenants.

The covenant refers to God graciously taking the initiative, and entering into a special relationship with men and women. The fact that the Creator of the universe is interested in the eternal welfare of His creatures, and promises and pledges Himself to be their God, at first seems almost too good to be true. But the Bible tells us it is so. The God Who cannot break His Word says: *I will be their God and they will be My people* (Jeremiah 31:33).

In Matthew 26:28, Jesus teaches us that when He died on the cross, His precious blood which was shed there was *the blood of the new covenant, which is poured out for many for the forgiveness of sins* - the very sins which prevent us from having any relationship with God at all.

In Numbers 18:19, God speaks of *a covenant of salt for ever . . .* A commentator said of this:-

> Salt was often used among oriental peoples for ratifying agreements, so that salt became a symbol of fidelity and constancy.

So next time you sprinkle salt on your meal, remind yourself of God's constancy and faithfulness to His people in the Lord Jesus Christ. His love is a love that will not let us go.

2. The Salt of the Christ

Food without salt is tasteless for sure. But life without Christ is even more so. It is only by knowing Jesus as our own, personal Saviour that we really begin to live, and not just exist. The hymn says ' solid joys and lasting treasures, none but Zion's children know.' And it is right. The best of this world's treasure and pleasure will eventually fade away. But listen to the promise of Jesus: *'I came that they may have life and have it abundantly'* (John 10:10).

Salt also reminds us of Christ's sinlessness and incorruptibility. In Biblical times, they had no deep freezers or canning factories, and so one of the few ways of preserving food in that hot climate was by rubbing it with salt. Without salt, in those days, food would soon go bad.

Death is the ultimate bad experience. Death, of course, brings decay. Jesus, however, the sinless One, was not subject to the law of sin and death. Hence Peter, on the day of Pentecost, proclaimed how the Psalmist had previously predicted of the coming Christ: *Thou wilt not abandon My soul to Hades or let Thy Holy One see corruption . . . . He foresaw and spoke of the resurrection of Christ, that He was not abandoned to Hades, nor did His flesh see corruption* (Acts 2:27,32).

So salt reminds us of Christ's resurrection from the dead. He did not rot in the grave. He was *raised on the third day in accordance with the Scriptures* (1 Corinthians 15:4). His resurrection proves that He is God. His resurrection proves that our sins are forgiven - for it shows that God accepted the perfect sacrifice Christ made on behalf of sinners. His resurrection also is the promise that all who belong to Christ will, one day, possess a glorious resurrection body like His, in the new heavens and new earth - *the Lord Jesus Christ, . . . will change our lowly body to be like His glorious body, by the power which enables Him even to subject all things to Himself* (Philippians 3:21).

3. The Salt of the Christian

In Matthew 5:13, Jesus says to His disciples in every age: *You are the salt of the earth.*

If we are Christians then, we are salt and we are to be salt! We are to remember that we are God's people, and to walk in His love and light day by day, rejoicing that nothing can separate us from His covenant love.

Salt also reminds us that we are called to be holy and pure, seeking the help of God's Holy Spirit to be so. *For this is the will of God, your sanctification . . .* (1 Thessalonians 4:3). A Christian who lives a holy life is a powerful testimony in this unholy world. A Christian characterised by holiness has a cleansing, preserving influence on the non Christians who witnesses such a life. Church history reveals just how in debt the world is to Christians who live out their salvation in a 'secular' setting, giving others a thirst for Jesus, the One Who alone provides the living water of life (John 4:14,7:37).

A Christian is also commanded to be 'salty' in his or her talk as well as his or her walk. Paul said: *Let your speech always be gracious, seasoned with salt* (Colossians 4:6). What we say reflects who we are. What we say reveals our innermost heart. If we really know God's love in Christ, it cannot but come out in our speech - we will long to share the Gospel with others too.

So there are some lessons from the salt cellar. There is the salt of God's covenant - God's loving and absolute commitment to us for our blessing. There is the salt of Christ - the flavour He alone can bring to our lives, as well as reminding us of His purity and His incorruptibility. And there is also the salt of the Christian, for Jesus said *You are the salt of the earth*. When we know God in Christ is committed to us in covenant love, a response to Him is demanded and required. A good prayer to pray in this respect is:-

> Have Thine Own way Lord, have Thine Own way
> Hold o'er my being absolute sway
> Fill with Thy Spirit till all shall see
> Christ only, always, living in me.

25

BY BLUE GALILEE

One of the most breathtakingly beautiful places on God's earth I have ever seen has to be the Sea of Galilee in northern Israel. I was only there for five days, but it made a lasting impact and impression. It all came back to me the other evening when I showed some friends my slides of my visit to the Holy Land. I gave them a quick forty minute tour of Israel, 'walking in the footsteps of Jesus', all from the comfort of an armchair.

For the Christian, the Sea of Galilee is sanctified by its association with the life and ministry of Jesus. That freshwater lake figures large in the Gospel records. For this chapter, let us think about some of the times it is mentioned:-

The Call to Follow Jesus

In Mark 1:16 we read: *And passing along by the Sea of Galilee, He (Jesus) saw Simon and Andrew the brother of Simon casting a net in the sea, for they were fishermen. And Jesus said to them 'Follow Me and I will make you fishers of men.' And immediately they left their nets and followed Him.*

This goes to show that the Christian Faith is an evangelistic Faith. It seeks, as it were, to catch men and women for Christ. If we are Christians, we will have eternal cause to be grateful that by God's grace we were ever caught in the Gospel net - rescued from eternal danger and saved for eternal life in God's kingdom. Having been saved - that is, having tasted of the joy of God's salvation - it is natural that we also will want to share the Gospel and lead others into the joy of God's salvation too. Even if we are not called into full-time Gospel ministry like those Galilean fishermen were, we certainly will want to emulate their spirit:-

Boats and nets they left behind them
Those disciples by the lake
Christ to follow, He would teach them
Men alive henceforth to take

We must follow this same Master
If we also souls would win
Faithfully proclaim the Gospel
Snatching men from hell and sin.

Walking on the Water

Amazingly, the Gospel records record as a matter of plain fact, that the Lord Jesus had the ability actually to walk on the waters of the Sea of Galilee without sinking. Matthew 14:25 ff. reads:-

And in the fourth watch of the night He (Jesus) came to them (the disciples), walking on the sea. But when the disciples saw Him walking on the sea, they were terrified, saying, 'It is a ghost!' And they cried out for fear. But immediately He spoke to them saying 'Take heart, it is I; have no fear.'

Cynics and sceptics have suggested that the Lord Jesus was not really walking on the water here. No, they say. He was only walking on sandbanks. The difficulty with this view though is that the freshwater lake of the Sea of Galilee does not actually have any sandbanks!

Jesus' ability to walk on water might justly amaze and astonish us. But it is a small matter to Almighty God. In this incident, Jesus was demonstrating His deity - His absolute lordship over His creation. John opens his Gospel by reminding us of Christ's agency in the creation of the universe: *In the beginning was the Word, and the Word was with God, and the Word was God. He was in the beginning with God; all things were made through Him and without Him was not anything made that was made* (John 1:1-3). Jesus' walking on the water amazes us as it amazed His disciples. Yet it should not. For here we are dealing with no mere man. He we are brought face to face with the Creator-God - God in the flesh.

Calming the Sea : Calming the Soul

Another demonstration of Christ's deity occurred on the Sea of Galilee during a frightening storm. The Sea of Galilee is known for its sudden storms and squalls. Its geography and topography makes it susceptible to these. Luke records how on one occasion, Jesus and His disciples:-

. . . Set out and as they sailed He fell asleep. And a storm of wind came down on the lake and they were filling with water and were in danger. And they went and woke Him saying 'Master, Master, we are perishing!' And He awoke and rebuked the wind and the raging waves, and they ceased and there was a great calm (Luke 8:22 ff.).

There it is. It is a miracle - but if we believe in God, miracles present no difficulty. After it occurred, the disciples made an exclamation: *'Who then is this, that He commands even wind and water, and they obey Him?'* (Luke 8:25). This is none other than God in the flesh. The Psalmist had already written of God: *Thou dost rule the raging of the sea; when its waves rise, Thou stillest them* (Psalm 89:9).

By way of application, we may be assured of Jesus' presence with us in the storms of life. None of the storms you and I face are too mighty for Him. He is just as able to calm a troubled soul today as He was able to calm the turbulent sea then. *Mightier than the thunders of many waters, mightier than the waves of the sea, the LORD on high is mighty* (Psalm 93:4).

The Risen Redeemer

Finally, the Sea of Galilee reminds us that Jesus is alive today. We serve a risen Saviour. John records that one of the resurrection appearances of Jesus was by this beautiful lake. John 21:1 ff.:-

Jesus revealed Himself again to the disciples by the Sea of Tiberius . . . The disciples were out on the lake again, back to their old fishing trade. Just as day was breaking, Jesus stood on the beach. That disciple whom Jesus loved said 'It is the Lord!' When Simon Peter heard that it was the Lord, he put on his clothes, for he was stripped for work, and sprang into the sea . . .

Jesus had risen from the dead! The resurrection of Christ is one of the basic fundamentals of the Christian Faith. He was *designated Son of God in power according to the Spirit of holiness by His resurrection from the dead, Jesus Christ our Lord* (Romans 1:4). The Sea of Galilee therefore brings to mind this one Fact that has changed the world for ever.

Beautiful, blue, tranquil, unspoilt Sea of Galilee. Once seen, it is never forgotten. But if we never have the privilege of going there, we still have an open Bible. In the Bible, the Sea of Galilee - as we have seen - gives us valuable lessons in evangelism, the power and love of Christ, and the life-changing Fact that Jesus is alive today.

Do you know the One Who made the Sea of Galilee so famous and really put it on the map? If not, there is no time like now to put your faith in Him, and become one of His disciples, safe in His care for time and eternity.

Those Galilean fishermen left all for Jesus, and they gained all by so doing. You and I are invited to do the same:-

In simple trust like theirs who heard
Beside the Syrian sea
The gracious calling of the Lord
Let us like them without a word
Rise up and follow Thee
Rise up and follow Thee.

26

FRIENDS

Under the word 'friend', the dictionary gives this definition: 'one joined to another in intimacy and affection; one who is on the same side; sympathiser, helper'. The definition is no doubt true, if a little cool and clinical. More anecdotally, a true friend is one who knows all about you, and stands by you through thick and thin.

It is difficult to get by without any friends. The best of physical health, and even the possession of great physical wealth all become a bit meaningless if all is not well with us in the sphere of our human, interpersonal relationships.

I, for one, find the topic of friendship difficult to discuss. I believe that the number of true friends that any of us have is actually quite small, as friends are not to be confused with associates and acquaintances. For some of us, forming friendships is difficult, as past, hard experience has taught us not to be too open with everyone, as this can leave us vulnerable to getting hurt.

The Puritans used to talk about a 'soul friend' or a 'bosom friend'. By this they meant one particular friend and confidante who is especially close. If you have one of these, thank God for such a friendship, value it and guard it. Even the Lord Jesus Christ Himself, whilst being acquainted with many, chose twelve disciples. Of these twelve, three seemed closer to Him than the others, and of these inner three, John seemed to be the closest. John was literally Jesus' 'bosom friend'- *One of His disciples, whom Jesus loved, was lying close to the breast of Jesus* (John 13:23).

Friendship in the Bible

Have you ever thought that the Bible can be considered as a friendship book? Human and divine relationships fill its pages. We read, for instance, in 1 Samuel 18:1 that *the soul of Jonathan was knit to the soul of David, and Jonathan loved him as his own soul.* In the Old Testament we also read of Daniel and his three companions: all four stuck together and remained faithful to the true God in an environment of idolatry. Then in the New Testament we can glimpse something of the friendship and fellowship between Paul and my namesake Timothy. Romans 16 contains a catalogue of Paul's Christian friends in Rome - the chapter oozes affection.

Psalm 41:9 though reads like this: *Even My bosom friend in whom I trusted, who ate of My bread, has lifted his heel against Me.* The reference seems to be a prophetic one of Judas Iscariot's betrayal of Jesus. It is a sobering warning that friends have the capability of letting us down and disappointing us - as Bishop Ryle put it: 'The best of men are men at best.' Similarly, in Psalm 55:12 ff., David, with great sorrow, tells how the hurts from a supposed friend are far harder to take than the barbs of an enemy. . .

The Bible then contains the stories of many human relationships. All life is there. Yet the over-riding message of the Bible is the staggering truth that men and women - ordinary, sinful men and women like you and me - can come into a relationship with and know the friendship of, none less than Almighty God Himself.

The Friendship of God

The friendship of the LORD is for those who fear Him, and He makes known to them His covenant (Psalm 25:14). We saw in our chapter on

'Salt' that the word 'Covenant' is one of the key words of the Bible. God's covenant refers to His unbreakable pledge and promise to remain faithful to us and be our God through life, death and all eternity.

James 2:23 says that *Abraham believed God and it was reckoned to him as righteousness; and he was called the friend of God.* It is staggering to think that Abraham is described as *the friend of God* , but the Bible tells us so. Abraham was the founder of the Hebrew race, and also, in a spiritual sense, the father of all Christians, as we read in Galatians 3:29 that *if you are Christ's, then you are Abraham's offspring, heirs according to promise.* Putting this together, we can state that we too can know God as our friend if we trust Him, just like Abraham did. Abraham was far from perfect, just as we are far from perfect. But if we trust in God, and believe His promise of salvation in the Lord Jesus Christ, we too will be declared righteous by God on behalf of the Lord Jesus, and we too can then know the friendship of God.

Christ, the Incomparable Friend

In John 15:13 ff., Jesus said *'Greater love has no man than this, that a man lay down his life for his friends. You are My friends if you do what I command you'* Jesus did, of course, lay down His life for His friends. But He did more than that. He laid down His life for His enemies. The Bible says *God shows His love for us in that while we were yet sinners Christ died for us . . . While we were enemies we were reconciled to God by the death of His Son* (Romans 5:8,10).

It is our sin which makes us God's enemies. We are all sinners by nature, and so a thrice holy God can only be opposed to us. The marvel of the Gospel though is the Good News that God loved sinners so much that He found a way for them to be reconciled to Himself. God sent His Own Son, the Lord Jesus Christ to die the death of the cross, so that we might be able to know God's pardon, peace and eternal friendship and fellowship.

Few would deny that friends are a highly desirable 'commodity' to have. Unfortunately though, human friendships may have failure and disappointment built into them, for they are only human. The friendship of God through Jesus Christ though is on an altogether different scale. He is the God of the covenant. He is faithful and will not fail. *There are friends who pretend to be friends, but there is a Friend who sticks closer than a brother* (Proverbs 17:24). *He has said, 'I will never fail you nor forsake you'* (Hebrews 13:5).

I've found a Friend, O such a Friend!
He loved me e're I knew Him
He drew me with the cords of love
And thus He bound me to Him
And round my heart still closely twine
Those ties which nought can sever
For I am Christ's, and He is mine
For ever and for ever.

27

THE GOD OF THE ELDERLY
Even to your old age I am He, and to grey hairs I will carry you
(Isaiah 46:4).

I recently heard someone use the word 'wrinkly' to describe someone who is old, and the word really grated on me. Relatively speaking, as a 'thirty something', I am not yet all that old. I found the word somewhat offensive though, as I have benefited a great deal, over my years, from the ministry of some experienced saints of God, who, although advanced in years have remained very youthful in spirit. Also, it may not have occurred to the employer of the word 'wrinkly' that he himself might be in that category one day.

The Fashion of the Day

Today, and possibly since the late 1950's and 1960's, the general emphasis is on the young and youthfulness. The advertising industry does not generally have much time for those who are over twenty five. Few old people are used to sell products. Yet when we turn to the Bible, we see that the emphasis is completely contrary to the trend of today. In the Bible, it was 'chic and trendy', not to be young, but to be old. Let us explore this a little further:-

Back to the Bible

Proverbs 16:31 reads: *A hoary head* (that is, a white/grey head) *is a crown of glory; it is gained in a righteous life.* Think of that. Today, the hair-dye, and hair colour restoring industry is big business - but such an industry did not exist in Bible times, when grey hair was respected. In Bible times, grey/white hair was considered to epitomise wisdom and experience - and it is from this, we note in passing, that the tradition of our judges putting on white wigs stems.

Job 12:12 reads: *Wisdom is with the aged, and understanding in length of days.* Contrast this with a tongue in cheek definition of a teenager which goes 'Teenagers are people who are always ready to give adults the full benefits of their inexperience.' We may take this definition with a pinch of salt, as there are no doubt wise and astute teenagers, just as there are foolish and cantankerous old folks. Sin is no respecter of age or persons. Yet this apart, you can see the drift of the argument. This being so, maybe we could all take much better heed of the spirit, if not the letter of Leviticus 19:32: *You shall rise up before the hoary head, and honour the face of an old man, and you shall fear your God: I am the LORD.*

The Fruitfulness of Old Age

If we know the Bible - as well as trawling our personal experience - we will know that old age does not necessarily prevent people from working for the Lord in a full and fruitful manner. It is not generally very well known, for instance, that Moses was eighty years of age when, under the Lord, he led the people of Israel out of slavery in Egypt - an event central to the Old Testament revelation. Then we have the testimony of that active grandfather, Caleb, the one who *wholly followed the LORD my God* (Joshua 14:8,9). Caleb testified *I am this day eighty five years old, I am still as strong to this day as I was in the day that Moses sent me; my strength now is as my strength then, for war, and for going and coming* (Joshua 14:11)

Skipping the centuries, and turning to the New Testament, we come face to face with one old lady called Anna. Anna, we are told, was eighty four years old, yet *she did not depart from the temple, worshipping with fasting and prayer night and day* (Luke 2:37). Maybe Paul had Anna's type in mind, when he mentioned the widow who *continues in supplications and prayers night and day* (1 Timothy 5:5). What a work is prayer. Is there a higher occupation than true prayer? Only eternity will reveal the debt that the church and the world owes, not to famous people in prominent, public roles, but to the faithful, unseen prayers of those mature in years and perhaps infirm in body. Senior saint, is the Lord calling you to be an intercessor? Are you burdened to pray for the spread of the Gospel and those who proclaim it? Do you long for more and more people to enter into the joy of God's salvation which is yours in Christ? Do you not long for God's purposes of grace and glory to be fulfilled? In the mystery of providence, your prayers can play a major part in this.

The Ageless God

In a world obsessed with age, it is good to remind ourselves that God Himself never grows old. He is age-less. He is eternal - the great I AM and the everlasting 'now'. In Revelation 1:8 He says of Himself: *I am the Alpha and the Omega, . . . The Lord God, Who is and Who was and Who is to come, the Almighty.* And what is true of God is also true of His Son, for the Bible is clear that the Lord Jesus *continues as a priest for ever* (Hebrews 7:3) and is a *priest . . . by the power of an indestructible life . . . He holds His priesthood permanently because He continues for ever* (Hebrews 7:16,24). It is because this is so that the next verse can proclaim *Consequently He is able to save for all time those who draw near to God through Him, since He always lives to make intercession for them* (Hebrews 7:25).

The Christian's Endless Hope

Jesus saves for time and eternity. The good news for ageing saints and for Christians of all ages, is that in the glory land we will never grow old. The full Christian hope involves the redemption of the body as much as the salvation of the soul. Our eternal hope will see the end of all death, decay, disease and ageing - in fact an eradication of everything that currently brings us down. We just cannot conceive of the wonder of it, limited by time as we are, but the Bible tells us so!

> When we've been there ten thousand years
> Bright shining as the sun
> We've no less days to sing God's praise
> Than when we first began.

28

THE ICHTHUS - THE SIGN OF THE FISH

In our opening chapter, we considered the symbol of the anchor - a common symbol of the Christian Faith in the early church. Another popular symbol of those times however was that of the fish. It again was a secret symbol, as the Christian Faith was somewhat illicit until 313 AD, when the Emperor Constantine was converted. The fish symbol can still be seen in the ancient catacombs, but is not confined to the first century. Interestingly, the fish symbol has made something of a comeback amongst Christians in recent years. I have seen it as both a lapel badge and a car sticker. But why is the emblem of a fish used as a symbol of the Christian Faith?

It's all Greek

The New Testament was originally written in Greek, as this was the universal language of the first century. The Greek word for fish is ICHTHUS. In Greek, this is composed of five letters, namely iota, chi, theta, upsilon and sigma. From those five letters, the early Christians composed an acrostic, an acrostic which when translated into English reads JESUS CHRIST GOD'S SON SAVIOUR. So let us consider this acrostic further, and delve deeper into the meaning of the sign of the fish:-

Iota - Jesus

The first letter - iota - stands for 'Jesus'. It reminds us that the Christian Faith is centred on a Person, the Person of the Lord Jesus Christ. *Jesus is Lord* was one of the earliest Christian confessions and creeds - a confession which, incidentally often forfeited you your life, being diametrically opposed to the required confession 'Caesar is Lord' as it was.

The name 'Jesus' was a common one in Jewish circles. It is the same name as the Hebrew 'Joshua'. Joshua was a prominent character in the Old Testament, being the leader who succeeded Moses in leading the Israelites over the river Jordan into the Promised Land of Canaan. The name 'Jesus' means 'the Lord is salvation' or 'the Lord saves'. It reminds us of what Jesus came to do: *You shall call His name Jesus, for He will save His people from their sins* (Matthew 1:21). *Christ Jesus came into the world to save sinners* (1 Timothy 1:15).

It is Jesus alone Who saves us from our sins and leads us over the divide of death into the Promised Land - the incomparable land of heaven itself. Note the first letter of the fish then, Iota, standing for 'Jesus.' It is the theme of ten thousand hymns:-

> How sweet the name of Jesus sounds
> In a believer's ear
> It soothes his sorrows, heals his wounds
> And drives away his fear.

Chi - Christ

The second letter of the fish acrostic is chi, standing for Christos or Christ. Christ is a title rather than a name. To illustrate, consider Prince Philip. Philip is his name, but 'Prince' is a title.

'Christ' means 'the anointed one' or 'Messiah.' The Old Testament contains many Messianic promises and prophecies. How the Jews longed for the Anointed One - One sent by God Who would come and bring in the Kingdom of Heaven. In Jesus He arrived! *'You are the Christ, the Son of the living God'* (Matthew 16:16) confessed Peter to Jesus. But did Jesus believe Himself to be the Messiah? Scripture records that He did. In John 4:25 a woman of Samaria mused to Jesus: *'I know that Messiah is coming' (He Who is called Christ)* and in the next verse we read that *Jesus said to her, 'I Who speak to you am He.'* Rightly and joyfully therefore Christians sing the lovely hymn of praise to Jesus which goes:-

> Hail to the Lord's anointed
> Great David's Greater Son
> Hail in the time appointed
> His reign on earth begun!
> He comes to break oppression
> To set the captives free
> To take away transgression
> And rule in equity.

Theta and Upsilon - God's Son

The third and fourth letters of the fish acrostic, theta and upsilon, stand for 'God's Son' or 'Son of God.' We see here that, whilst Jesus was certainly fully human, He was more than just a mere man. He was and is the unique, one and only, only begotten Son of God. Consider Peter's confession once again. He said to Jesus *'You are the Christ, the Son of the living God'*. Similarly, at Jesus' baptism, Matthew records the following remarkable occurrence: *lo, a voice from heaven, saying 'This is My beloved Son, with Whom I am well pleased'* (Matthew 3:17). We may disagree with Peter, as he was a fallible human being. But who would dare disagree with the voice from heaven as regards the identity of Christ? Doing so would surely be the height of folly and soul damning arrogance.

That Jesus is the Son of God and God the Son - the Second Person of the blessed Trinity - is a Fundamental of the Christian

Faith. Those who deny the deity of Christ, that is, those who cast aspersions on His identity as the eternal Son of God, are not and can never be Christians in the Biblical sense of the word 'Christian'.

Before the Apostle Paul's conversion, he was one of the most ardent adherents of the Jewish Faith you could find. In his own words: *I advanced in Judaism beyond many of my own age among my people, so extremely zealous was I for the traditions of my fathers* (Galatians 1:14). As a good Jew, he was adamant that worshipping Jesus was idolatry, for only God Himself is to be worshipped. But how all this changed when the true identity of Jesus was revealed to Paul at his conversion. Acts 9:20 records of Paul that, no sooner had he been converted than *in the synagogues immediately he proclaimed Jesus saying 'He is the Son of God.'*

Sigma - Saviour

The last letter of the fish acrostic is sigma, standing for 'Saviour'. So the last letter takes us back to where we began! *You shall call His name Jesus for He will save His people from their sins* (Matthew 1:21). *Christ Jesus came into the world to save sinners* (1 Timothy 1:15). *The Son of Man came to seek and to save the lost* (Luke 19:10).

As we are all sinners, it is a saviour that we need - not a teacher, or an example or a code of rules and regulations. In Jesus alone we have the Saviour for our need. He is the eternal Son of God. He came into the world to save sinners. He died on a cross to save sinners. He rose from the grave to save sinners. He ascended into heaven and sat down at the right hand of God where He continually intercedes for sinners. One day, He is coming again, and will take His people to Himself and every knee shall bow before Him. No one will cast doubt on His deity then.

So there is the sign of the fish or the ichthus - Jesus Christ God's Son Saviour. When I was visiting a hospital recently, I met a fellow believer quietly going about his business. I identified him by the little silver fish he wore on his lapel. When we know the true meaning of the sign of the fish, and have Jesus dwelling in our heart, we have just cause to wear such a fish sign with joy and pride.

29

'JUST MY CUP OF TEA'

In common with 99.9% of British people, I say that nothing beats a good, strong, hot cup of tea. For me, any time is tea time - the morning, afternoon, winter and summer. Interestingly, tea has a figurative meaning in our language as well as a literal one. When people don't like something they sometimes say: 'It's not my cup of tea at all.'

Did you know that the Bible also uses the picture of a 'cup' to describe what happens to us in this life? In the Bible, the word 'cup' is used figuratively to describe both blessing and suffering. Few would deny that life is made up of both, so let us explore this a little further. Let us look at some Bible cups:-

The Cup of Blessing

In Psalm 16:5, David wrote: *The LORD is my chosen portion and my cup.* Here we have the cup of blessing. Knowing God is surely the greatest blessing of all. It is a blessing which is literally 'out of this world', for this world cannot bestow such a blessing upon us, and thankfully, this world cannot take away this incomparable blessing from us. Jesus said: *This is eternal life, that they know Thee the only true God, and Jesus Christ Whom Thou hast sent* (John 17:3). It is through Jesus that we know God. He is God in the flesh, and His death on the cross alone reconciles us to God the Father, and so gives us fellowship with Him - fellowship with the One Who is the fount of every blessing; the 'God from Whom all blessings flow.'

The Cup of Christ's Suffering

With great solemnity, we note that the cup of suffering figured prominently in the life of the Lord Jesus Christ. As He considered His impending death on the cross, Jesus prayed to His Father: *'Father, if Thou art willing, remove this cup from Me; nevertheless not My will, but Thine, be done'* (Luke 22:42). With our complete New Testament hindsight, we know that it was the will of God that Jesus should drink the cup of suffering on Calvary's cross - and drink it in full.

Before He was nailed cruelly to the cross, there was one literal cup which Jesus refused. Mark 15:22 ff. records: *they brought Him to the place called Golgotha (which means the place of a skull). And they offered Him wine mingled with myrrh; but He did not take it.* This 'wine mingled with myrrh' would have acted as a painkilling sedative. But Jesus declined it. He died the cruel death of Calvary with all His physical and mental faculties totally clear and intact.

The Cup of Wrath

The question is: Why did Jesus shrink from drinking the cup of suffering, and pray to God for its removal in Gethsemane's garden? The martyrs, for instance, who subsequently died in Jesus' name, faced their deaths with much more fortitude - even joy. The answer to the question is found by looking beyond the physical sufferings of Jesus - excruciating though they were - to His spiritual sufferings.

The 'cup', in Scripture, can also refer to the wrath of God. The wrath of God is the most fearful reality of all, and in Gethsemane,

Jesus contemplated drinking this bitterest of cups. That the 'cup' refers to the wrath of God is plain from the following Scriptures:-

For in the hand of the LORD there is a cup, with foaming wine, well mixed, and He will pour a draught from it, and all the wicked of the earth shall drain it down to the dregs (Psalm 75:8).

Thus the LORD, the God of Israel, said to me: 'Take from My hand this cup of the wine of wrath . . . (Jeremiah 25:15).

On the cross then, Jesus stood in the sinner's stead and endured the wrath of God. He was cursed so that we might be blessed. His cry was *'My God, My God, why hast Thou forsaken Me?'* (Matthew 27:46). At Calvary He drank the cup of damnation. At Calvary, He drained the cup of damnation dry for all who recognise their sin and guilt, and cast themselves on the crucified Saviour for deliverance. *Since, therefore, we are now justified by His blood, much more shall we be saved by Him from the wrath of God* (Romans 5:9).Which leads us finally to:-

The Cup of Salvation

In the most joyful of tones, Psalm 116:12,13 rings out as follows:-
What shall I render to the LORD for all His bounty to me? I will lift up the cup of salvation and call on the name of the LORD. The cup of salvation! As a chorus goes: 'Come and taste the new wine, the wine of the kingdom of God.'

The Christian rejoices in a present salvation - the forgiveness of sins, peace with God and fellowship with God through and because of our Lord Jesus Christ. But a Christian also anticipates a consummated salvation - there is even better wine to come! At the first Lord's Supper, Jesus took a cup and said *'This is My blood of the new covenant, which is poured out for many for the forgiveness of sins. I tell you I shall not drink again of the fruit of the vine until that day when I drink it new with you in My Father's kingdom'* (Matthew 26:28,29). A cup of glory most certainly awaits all who belong to Jesus. *Blessed are those who are invited to the marriage supper of the Lamb* (Revelation 19:9).

So there are some of the cups, literal and metaphorical of the Bible. Note them well. There is a verse from a hymn which sums up much of what we have considered in this chapter about Bible cups rather wonderfully. It goes:-

> Death and the curse were in our cup
> O Christ 'twas full for Thee
> But Thou hast drained the last dark drop
> 'Tis empty now for me
> That bitter cup, love drank it up
> Now blessings draught for me.

30

THERE'S NO PLACE LIKE HOME

We never know what a day may bring forth - to paraphrase the Scripture of James 4:14. My carefully laid plans for Christmas 2002 - which included a sponsored swim in the sea - were changed rather suddenly and dramatically by an unplanned and unbudgeted for emergency visit to hospital at precisely 3.30 am, the second Saturday before Christmas. Surreal was the word. I hoped that I was dreaming, but knew I was not. I ended up being off work for ten days, and stayed with my parents and their cat, just like old times. There is, truth be told, no place like home. It is a place where there is no pretence, but only love and acceptance for who we are, rather than what we do, or the role we play, or an image we project. For over a week, I had the privilege of sleeping in the bedroom of my boyhood!

The Prodigal Returns

Did you know that one of the ways in which the Bible depicts salvation, is by using the picture of coming home? There is a famous parable, told by Jesus in Luke 15, known as 'The Parable of the Prodigal Son.' In it, a rebellious boy wandered far from home and, to his cost, sought happiness in all the pleasures - licit and illicit - that this world has to offer. It was fine for a time, but then *he began to be in want* (Luke 15:14). He ended up as a slave, with pigs for company. Such is not exactly the high-life for a Jewish boy, yet, ceremonially unclean though they were, he envied the pigs. At least they were not hungry, but he was. *But when he came to himself . . .* (Luke 15:17), continues the parable in a major turning point, the prodigal saw sense. He realised just how much better off he would be at home. So he 'upped and offed' and went home, humbled in spirit and repentant in heart. When he arrived home, he was warmly embraced by his father who called out for a celebration. *'For this my son was dead and is alive again; he was lost, and is found'* (Luke 15:24).

Going Home

We can view the 'Parable of the Prodigal Son' from more than one angle, but for this final chapter, let us consider its teaching on salvation as a 'going home'.

We are designed for fellowship with God our Maker. God Himself is our true 'heart's home'. Yet our sin separates us from God. Sin also renders us liable to God's judgement. And sin also makes us very unhappy, cutting us off from our home, and giving us that restless, hopeless, dissatisfied, rootless feeling as a consequence.

The Gospel of Christ though is the Good News that, by the grace of God, we may return home. Christ died that our sins might be forgiven and so we might be restored to fellowship with God for time and eternity. Now we can see why repentance is such an integral part of the Gospel from our perspective. Repentance is a turning back to God. Once we repent and turn to Him, just like the Prodigal, we will be received warmly by Him, for the sake of His Son.

Luke closes his book showing how *He (Jesus) opened their minds to understand the Scriptures, and He said to them ' Thus it is written, that the Christ should suffer and on the third day rise from the dead, and that* repentance *and forgiveness of sins should be preached in His name to all nations* (Luke 24:45-47). Did you notice the word 'repentance' there? Repentance is a going home. Or, more technically:-

> Repentance unto life is a saving grace whereby a sinner, out of a true sense of his sin and apprehension of the grace of God in Christ doth with grief and hatred of his sin turn from it unto God, with full purpose of and endeavour after new obedience (*Shorter Catechism*).

At Home

When *our fellowship is with the Father and with His Son Jesus Christ* (1 John 1:3) we truly may be said to be 'at home.' There is no place like home. It cannot be bettered. The Psalmist said to God: *Whom have I in heaven but Thee? And there is nothing upon earth that I desire besides Thee. My flesh and my heart may fail, but God is the strength of my heart and my portion for ever* (Psalm 73:25,26).

The glorious Gospel of the Christian Church then is 'A warm welcome to Jesus.' It presses the following crucial question on all those who are strangers to the redeeming work of Christ for sinners on the cross. It asks gently:-

> Are you coming Home ye wanderers
> Whom Jesus died to win -
> All footsore lame and weary
> Your garments stained with sin?
> Will you seek the blood of Jesus
> To wash your garments white?
> Will you trust His precious promise
> Are you coming home tonight?
>
> Are you coming Home ye lost ones
> Behold, your Lord doth wait
> Come then! No longer linger
> Come ere it be too late!

Will you come and let Him save you?
Oh, trust His love and might!
Will you come while He is calling
Are you coming Home tonight?

Soli Deo Gloria